Affects, Actions and Passions in Spinoza

Titles available

Affects, Actions and Passions in Spinoza: The Unity of Body and Mind,
Chantal Jaquet, translated by Tatiana Reznichenko

Forthcoming titles

Affirmation and Resistance in Spinoza: Strategy of the Conatus, Laurent
Bove, translated and edited by Émilie Filion-Donato and Hasana Sharp

The Machiavelli-Spinoza Encounter: Time and Occasion, Vittorio Morfino,
translated by Dave Mesing

Politics, Ontology and Knowledge in Spinoza, Alexandre Matheron,
translated and edited by Filippo Del Lucchese, David Maruzzella and Gil
Morejón

Experience and Eternity in Spinoza, Pierre-François Moreau, translated by
Robert Boncardo

Affects, Actions and Passions in Spinoza

The Unity of Body and Mind

Chantal Jaquet

Translated into English by Tatiana Reznichenko

EDINBURGH
University Press

Edinburgh University Press is one of the leading university presses in the UK. We publish academic books and journals in our selected subject areas across the humanities and social sciences, combining cutting-edge scholarship with high editorial and production values to produce academic works of lasting importance. For more information visit our website: edinburghuniversitypress.com

Edinburgh University Press Ltd
The Tun – Holyrood Road, 12(2f) Jackson's Entry, Edinburgh EH8 8PJ

Typeset in 10/12 Goudy Old Style by
Servis Filmsetting Ltd, Stockport, Cheshire,
and printed and bound in Great Britain.

A CIP record for this book is available from the British Library

ISBN 978 1 4744 3318 1 (hardback)
ISBN 978 1 4744 3320 4 (webready PDF)
ISBN 978 1 4744 3321 1 (epub)

Published with the support of the University of Edinburgh Scholarly Publishing Initiatives Fund.

Contents

Abbreviations   vi

Introduction   1

1. The Nature of the Union of Mind and Body in Spinoza   9

2. Spinoza's Break with Descartes Regarding the Affects in
   Ethics III   27

3. The Different Origins of the Affects in the Preface to
   the *Theological-Political Treatise* and in the *Ethics*   47

4. The Definition of 'Affect' in *Ethics* III   75

5. Variations of the Mixed Discourse   135

Conclusion   153

Bibliography   161
Index   168

Abbreviations

The following abbreviations are used:

Alt. Dem.	Alternative Demonstration
App.	Appendix
Ax.	Axiom
Cor.	Corollary
DA #	Definitions of the Affects
Def.	Definition
Dem.	Demonstration
Exp.	Explanation
Lem.	Lemma
NS	From the Curley translation of Spinoza, referring to a posthumous edition of 1677, *De Nagelate Schriften van B.D.S.*
Post.	Postulate
Praef.	Preface
Schol.	Scholium

AT	Adam and Tannery's *Œuvres de Descartes* (1909)
CWS	*The Collected Works of Spinoza*, trans. Edward Curley, cited by volume and page number
KV	*Short Treatise on God, Man, and His Well-Being* (*Korte Verhandeling*; e.g. KV II, 2, 2 refers to Part II, Chapter 2, Section 2)
PP	*Descartes'* Principles of Philosophy (*Principia philosophiae cartesianae*)

TdIE	*Treatise on the Emendation of the Intellect* (*Tractatus de Intellectus Emendatione*; references in brackets are to paragraph numbers, as introduced by Bruder)
TP	*Political Treatise* (*Tractatus politicus*; e.g. *TP* I, 5 refers to Chapter 1, paragraph 5)
TTP	*Theological-Political Treatise* (*Tractatus theologico-politicus*; e.g. *TTP* XVII, 7 refers to Chapter 17, paragraph 7, where the paragraph number corresponds to the Bruder edition, reproduced in Curley's *Collected Works, Volume II*)
TN	Translator's note

References to Spinoza's works cite paragraph or section numbers from Curley's translations, which have been used systematically in this volume to ensure consistency. I have signaled in the footnotes when Curley's translation has been altered.

Introduction

The renowned American neurologist Antonio R. Damasio, in his book *Looking for Spinoza: Joy, Sorrow and the Feeling Brain* (2003), explores what the great Dutch philosopher Baruch Spinoza can teach us about the nature of feelings. Having critiqued Descartes in his previous book *Descartes' Error* (1994), Damasio, head of the department of neurology at the University of Iowa Medical Center, positions himself firmly in the Spinozan camp (*Spinoza avait raison*[1] – 'Spinoza was right' – is the title of the French translation of the work) in order to shed light on the psychophysical processes brought into play by feelings. Damasio regards Spinoza as a precursor of modern neurobiology and confesses:

> Spinoza dealt with the subjects that preoccupy me most as a scientist – the nature of emotions and feelings and the relation of mind to body – and those same subjects have preoccupied many other thinkers of the past. To my eyes, however, he seemed to have prefigured solutions that researchers are now offering on a number of these issues. That was surprising.[2]

This interest in the Spinozan conception of the mind–body relationship is not an isolated phenomenon. It goes well beyond the current infatuation of American neurologists because it is shared by a number of French researchers, including Jean-Pierre

---

[1] French translation published by Odile Jacob, 2003.
[2] *Looking for Spinoza*, p. 11.

Changeux, the author of *Neuronal Man*, in which he claims a line of descent from Spinoza in his dialogue with Paul Ricoeur, *What Makes Us Think?* At the outset, he highlights the kinship between his own approach and that of Spinoza:

> While writing *Neuronal Man* I discovered Spinoza's *Ethics* and the full rigour of his thought. 'I shall consider human actions and appetites,' Spinoza says, 'just as if it were an investigation into lines, planes, or bodies.' Can anything more exciting be imagined than to try to reconstruct human life in a way that rejects teleology, that rejects anthropocentrism, that rejects all conceptions of the world that take shelter in religious superstition – what Spinoza called the 'refuge of ignorance'?[3]

Throughout the work, the Spinozan conception of the union of mind and body serves as both paradigm and common ground for a phenomenologist and a neurobiologist to tackle the difficult issue of the relationship between the brain and thought.[4] Jean-Pierre Changeux refers to Spinoza to support his idea of the primacy of the brain over the mind. If, for the author of the *Ethics*, ideas are a function of the body's affections, it is necessary to determine the physical structure of the brain and how its synaptic connections function, in order to shed light on the nature of thought.[5]

Yet references to the Spinozan conception of the psychophysical union go beyond the sphere of neurobiology to cover the entire field of biology. This is evidenced by Henri Atlan's *Is Science*

[3] *What Makes Us Think? A Neuroscientist and a Philosopher Argue about Ethics, Human Nature, and the Brain*, Jean-Pierre Changeux and Paul Ricoeur, trans. M. B. DeBevoise, p. 8.

[4] See my article, 'La référence à la conception spinoziste des rapports du corps et de l'esprit dans l'ouvrage de Paul Ricoeur et Jean-Pierre Changeux, *Ce qui nous fait penser, La Nature et la Règle*', in *Lectures contemporaines de Spinoza*, ed. P.-F. Moreau, M. Delbraccio and C. Cohen-Boulakia, Paris: Presses universitaires Paris Sorbonne, 2012.

[5] 'Whatever interpretation may be given to Spinoza's philosophy, I take from it the notion that reflective knowledge of our body, our brain and its functions (the soul) is fundamental to ethical reflection and moral judgement.' *What Makes Us Think?* p.23.

Inhuman?,[6] which takes an interest in the Dutch philosopher, as well as his numerous interventions paying homage to the author of the *Ethics*.[7] The success of the Spinozan model is not limited to the life sciences: it has also won over economics and the social sciences with the works of economists such as Frédéric Lordon, who has addressed the theory of the *conatus* and the mind and body's power of acting.[8] Without listing all of the current domains where Spinozan philosophy is influential, we must acknowledge the special attention that certain psychomotor specialists have been giving to Spinoza in recent years as part of an examination of their therapeutic practices. For example, Béatrice Vandewalle, Bruno Busschaert and Bernard Meurin[9] have been trying to establish a theory taking into account their knowledge and skills, on the basis of the principles governing the mind–body relationship described in *Ethics*.

The relevance of the Spinozan model, therefore, cannot be denied. It invites us to reflect on the impact and value of the current enthusiasm for it, a phenomenon historians of philosophy always eye with caution. Besides the issue of faddishness, invoking precursors or models is indeed often problematic because it is frequently based on second-hand knowledge and functions as a reference for the modern author rather than faithfully reproducing a thinker's philosophy. Antonio Damasio, for example, does not hide this, and on two occasions freely admits that he is not a philosopher and that his work is not about Spinoza's philosophy.[10]

It is therefore crucial to re-examine the issue of the mind–body

6 Published by Bayard, 2002. English translation available in Chapter 1 of Henri Atlan's *Selected Writings*, 2011.
7 See his article 'Théorie de l'action et identité psychophysique', in *Lectures contemporaines de Spinoza*, ed. P.-F. Moreau, M. Delbraccio and C. Cohen-Boulakia, Paris: Presses universitaires Paris Sorbonne, 2012.
8 See his article "Spinoza et le monde social," in *Lectures contemporaines de Spinoza*, ed. P.-F. Moreau, M. Delbraccio, C. Cohen-Boulakia, 2012.
9 See their lecture 'Des esprits animaux aux neurotransmetteurs, qui sait ce que peut le corps?' ('From animal spirits to neurotransmitters, who knows what the body is capable of?') at the 32nd annual 'Journées annuelles de thérapie psychomotrice' conference, *Corps et culture*, Lille, 2 October 2003.
10 See *Looking for Spinoza*, pp. 8 and 14–15.

relationship and its affective modalities in Spinoza from a philosophical angle, and explain them in the light of current thinking
in neurobiology, the social sciences and psychomotor education
in order to verify the relevance of interpretations of Spinoza's
thought. It is also critical to establish a precise and rigorous model
on the basis of an examination of the original texts, capable of
informing contemporary debates.

From this perspective, it is above all necessary to understand
what is problematic for researchers in the mind–body relationship
and what leads them to hail Spinoza as a pioneer. In *Looking for
Spinoza*, Antonio Damasio echoes the general preoccupations of
his contemporaries and sums them up in a series of questions:

> Are mind and body two different things or just one? If they are
> not the same, are mind and body made from two different sub-
> stances or just one? If there are two substances, does the mind
> substance come first and cause the body and its brain to exist, or
> does the body substance come first and its brain cause the mind?
> Also, how do those substances interact? [. . .] These are some of
> the main issues involved in the so-called mind–body problem, a
> problem whose solution is central to the understanding of who
> we are.[11]

Although these questions appear to have been resolved or
denounced as false problems in the eyes of many scientists and
philosophers, disagreement persists, which is sufficient evidence
for Damasio that the proposed solution is either unsatisfactory or
not well presented.

Admittedly, these problems are nothing new. They have
haunted mainstream philosophy since Descartes, who believed
that humans are composed of two substances: the soul or the thinking substance and the body or the extended substance. Indeed,
in his work the *Meditations on First Philosophy*, Descartes stated
that the union of an immaterial or non-extended substance and
a material or extended substance remains beyond understanding,
since the problem arises of whether they are able to interact. How

[11] *Looking for Spinoza*, p. 183.

can a material substance produce effects on an immaterial substance and vice versa? This is the key question Princess Elisabeth
of Bohemia asked Descartes in a letter dated 6 May 1643: 'So I ask
you please to tell me how the soul of a human being (it being only
a thinking substance) can determine the bodily spirits, in order to
bring about voluntary actions.'[12] The princess contended that all
determination of movement implied physical contact or a modification in extension and could hardly be explained by the action of
an immaterial and non-extended substance.

While emphasising Descartes' merits, Damasio reiterates the
princess's line of questioning and rejects the argument of the duality of substances and their mysterious interaction via the pineal
gland.[13] Psychophysical dualism has led scientists to a dead end.
That is why it is necessary to resort to other paradigms. Damasio
thus sees a solution to the problem Descartes left unresolved in the
Spinozan conception. He credits Spinoza with putting an end to
dualism by establishing the unity and identity of mind and body,
and by considering them to be parallel expressions of the same
substance:

> Whatever interpretation we favour for the pronouncements
> he made on the issue, we can be certain Spinoza was changing

---

[12] Princess Elisabeth of Bohemia and René Descartes, *The Correspondence
Between Princess Elisabeth of Bohemia and René Descartes*, Lisa Shapiro (ed.
and trans.), (Chicago: University of Chicago Press, 2007).

[13] 'In a bizarre twist, Descartes proposed that mind and body interacted,
but never explained how the interaction might take place beyond saying
that the pineal gland was the conduit for such interactions. The pineal
is a small structure located at the midline and base of the brain, and it
turns out to be rather poorly connected and endowed for the momentous
job Descartes required of it. In spite of Descartes' sophisticated views of
mental and physiological body processes, which he separately considered,
he either left the mutual connections of mind and body unspecified or
made them implausible. Princess Elizabeth of Bohemia, the sort of bright
and friendly student we all wish to have, saw quite clearly then what we
see clearly now: For mind and body to do the job Descartes required of
them, mind and body needed to make contact. However, by emptying
mind of any physical property, Descartes made contact impossible.' Ibid.,
p. 188.

the perspective he inherited from Descartes when he said, in *Ethics* Part I, that thought and extension, while distinguishable, are nonetheless attributes of the same substance, God or Nature. The reference to a single substance serves the purpose of claiming mind as inseparable from body, both created, somehow, from the same cloth. The reference to the two attributes, mind and body, acknowledged the distinction of two kinds of phenomena, a formulation that preserved an entirely sensible 'aspect' dualism, but rejected substance dualism. By placing thought and extension on equal footing, and by tying both to a single substance, Spinoza wished to overcome a problem that Descartes faced and failed to solve: the presence of two substances and the need to integrate them. On the face of it, Spinoza's solution no longer required mind and body to integrate or interact; mind and body would spring in parallel from the same substance, fully and mutually mimicking each other in their different manifestations. In a strict sense, the mind did not cause the body and the body did not cause the mind.[14]

Thus, what interests Damasio in Spinoza, in the first place, is his break with Descartes and his revolutionary vision of the mind–body relationship. He insists on this point on several occasions:[15]

What is Spinoza's insight, then? It is that mind and body are parallel and mutually correlated processes, mimicking each other at every crossroads, as two faces of the same thing. That

---

[14] Ibid. p. 209.

[15] 'Of great importance for what I shall be discussing was his notion that both the mind and the body were parallel attributes (call them manifestations) of the very same substance. At the very least, by refusing to ground mind and body on different substances, Spinoza was serving notice of his opposition to the view of the mind–body problem that prevailed in his time. His dissent stood out in a sea of conformity. More intriguing, however, was his notion that *the human mind is the idea of the human body*. This raised an arresting possibility. Spinoza might have intuited the principles behind the natural mechanisms responsible for the parallel manifestations of mind and body.' Ibid., p. 12.

deep inside these parallel phenomena there is a mechanism for representing bodily events in the mind.[16]

To be even more precise, it is the correspondence between mind and body that manifests itself in the affects and the pertinence of how they are treated that spurs Damasio to praise Spinoza's visionary genius:

> It is sensible to ask: why Spinoza? The short explanation is that Spinoza is thoroughly relevant to any discussion of human emotion and feeling. Spinoza saw drives, motivations, emotions, and feelings – an ensemble Spinoza called *affects* – as a central aspect of humanity. Joy and sorrow were two prominent concepts in his attempt to comprehend human beings and suggest ways in which their lives could be better lived.[17]

Under these circumstances, the analysis that needs to be carried out is quite clear: in response to the concerns of contemporary researchers, it will consist of examining the mind–body relationship through the lens of affects, and measuring the impact of Spinoza's break with Descartes on the subject. The key question, addressed in Chapter 1, is the exact nature of the mind–body relationship. Does the monism attributed to Spinoza really imply parallelism, as Antonio Damasio and Jean-Pierre Changeux believe, in line with many historians of philosophy? Once we have determined how the mind–body relationship is articulated, Chapter 2 will go on to analyse the causes of the break between the authors of the *Ethics* and *Meditations on First Philosophy*. In order to avoid perpetuating the simplistic model opposing Cartesian dualism with Spinozan monism, this approach will aim to understand how Spinoza himself perceived the break, and to make explicit the reasons Spinoza expressly put forward in *Ethics* Part III. It will then become possible, in Chapter 3, to reconstruct Spinoza's pioneering work in emotions by first studying how the concept of the affects was progressively developed, resulting in different

---

[16] *Looking for Spinoza*, p. 217.
[17] Ibid., p. 8.

origins of the affects in the *Theologico-Political Treatise* and in *Ethics*. Next, Chapter 4 analyses the complex definition of the *affectus*, and finally, Chapter 5 measures the psychophysical variations it produces.

1

The Nature of the Union of Mind and Body in Spinoza

The Essence of the Problem

For Spinoza, the human, consisting of a mind and a body, is not, however, a double being composed of two distinct entities. The mind and body must be thought of as a single unit, not as the conjunction of two extended and thinking substances. In fact, for him 'the Mind and the Body are one and the same Individual, which is conceived now under the attribute of thought, now under the attribute of Extension.'[1] Thus Spinoza rules out the possibility of dualism while establishing the possibility of a twofold mental and physical approach to human reality.

But if mind and body constitute one and the same being expressed in two ways, to understand human nature clearly and distinctly we need to understand how these two modes of conception interrelate and come together. The mind (*mens*), according to Spinoza, is neither a substance nor a receptacle nor a faculty. It is the idea of the body.[2] Therefore, the term *mens* describes nothing other than the perception or, more precisely, the conception that humans have of their own body – and by extension of the external world – through the various states affecting them. An idea, in fact, is defined as a concept the mind forms because it is a thinking thing.[3] By openly preferring the term 'conception'

---

[1] *Ethics* II, 21 Schol.; CWS I, 467–8.
[2] See *Ethics* II, 13; CWS I, 457.
[3] See *Ethics* II, Def. 3; CWS I, 447.

to 'perception', Spinoza emphasises the active, dynamic nature of the power of thought operating in the production of ideas.[4] Consequently, the mind is a way of conceptualising the body or forming an idea of it that is more or less adequate, depending on whether the affections modifying it are of a clear or confused nature.

By identifying the mind with the idea of the body, Spinoza provides guidance on how to conceptualise their relationship. He invites the reader to think of their union according to the model of the idea and its object. After establishing in Proposition 13 in Part II of the *Ethics* that 'the object of the idea constituting the human Mind is the Body', he concludes in the Scholium that 'from these [propositions] we understand not only that the human Mind is united to the Body, but also what should be understood by the union of Mind and Body'. The nature of the union between an idea and its object, however, is not self-evident. What does the argument that the mind is united to the body, as an idea is to its object, mean exactly?

To illustrate the nature of this relationship, Spinoza uses the geometrical example of a circle. 'A circle existing in nature and the idea of the existing circle, which is also in God, are one and the same thing, which is explained through different attributes.'[5] The circle is a mode of extension made by rotating a line segment with one end point fixed in space and the other mobile, and has the property of having equal radii. The idea of a circle is a mode of thought, which is formed on the basis of the idea of a line segment, and which includes the idea of equal radii. The circle and the idea of a circle are not, however, two different beings. It is the same individual that is conceived sometimes as a mode of extension, that is, the circle, and sometimes as a mode of thought, that is, the idea of a circle. The same applies to all bodies in nature and their ideas. The tree and the idea of a tree are not two different beings, but refer to one and the same thing considered alternately as an extended material reality and as the object of a thought. The

---

[4] See Def. 3, Exp.; *CWS* I, 447.
[5] *Ethics* II, 7 Schol.; *CWS* I, 451–2.

ideas of the circle, the tree or the human body objectively[6] contain all that the circle, tree or the human body contain formally. For Spinoza, all things have a formal essence that expresses their reality and an objective essence that is the idea of this reality. The objective essence, therefore, is nothing other than the idea of that thing, and is different from the formal essence, which applies to the thing in its material reality or its form. The mind, as an idea, is therefore the objective essence of the body. That is, as an object of thought it comprises everything that the essence of the body comprises formally or in reality, according to the same order and the same connection. If the form of the body, for example, is affected by Peter's presence and then by Paul's, the mind will successively have the idea of the body affected by Peter and then by Paul. The idea and its ideation are therefore identical and indivisible.

This identity, however, does not exclude alterity. Although they express one and the same thing, conceived now under the attribute of extension and now under the attribute of thought, the circle and the idea of a circle cannot necessarily be reduced to each other. The circle is a mode of extension, determined solely by modes of extension. The idea of a circle is a mode of thought, determined solely by modes of thought. Since it is distinct from its object, it has its own formal essence and can in turn become the object of an idea. This is what [33] of the *Treatise on the Emendation of the Intellect* highlights:

> For a circle is one thing and the idea of a circle another – the idea of a circle is not something which has a circumference and a centre, as a circle does. Nor is an idea of a body that body itself.

---

[6] The term 'objectively', borrowed from scholastic terminology, should not be understood as the opposite of 'subjectively'. It describes the fact that a thing is taken as the object of thought and refers to the representation or the conception the mind makes of it. Thus, for Descartes, 'objectively' is synonymous with 'by representation' and is distinguished from 'formally', which means 'really' or 'in actuality'. See *Meditations III* (AT, p. 33), p. 29: 'a thing exists objectively {or representatively} in the intellect by way of an idea'; see also p. 28.

Just like the circle and the idea of a circle, the mind and the body are two expressions of one and the same thing, but these two expressions are not strictly reducible to each other. An idea expresses the properties of its object, without necessarily having the same properties. Under these circumstances, the crux of the problem is to pinpoint the essence of this psychophysical union, which implies both the identity and the difference between mind and body, and to determine with precision how it is expressed.

Doing Away with Parallelism

Building on Proposition 7 of Part II, which establishes that 'the order and connection of ideas is the same (*idem est*) as the order and connection of things', commentators have come to consider identity tantamount to a form of parallelism between the sequence of ideas and the sequence of things and to conceptualise the psychophysical union and the correlation between physical and mental states on the basis of this model, seeing that the mind and body are united like an idea to its object.[7] This doctrine is well known as Leibniz's brainchild[8] but it is often presented as expressing Spinoza's thinking, even though it was imported retrospectively into his system, where, technically, it does not appear.

Martial Gueroult, while emphasising that in Proposition 7 'there it is less a parallelism than an identity between the two orders,'[9] nevertheless adopts Leibniz's argument. He deduces not only the existence of an extra-cogitative parallelism governing the

---

[7] See *Ethics* II, 13; CWS I, 457.

[8] See 'Reflections on the Doctrine of a Single Universal Spirit' [1702], in Leroy E. Loemker (trans. and ed.), *Philosophical Papers and Letters*, 2nd edn (Dordrecht: Kluwer, 1989), p. 556: 'I have established a perfect parallelism between what happens in the soul and what takes place in matter. I have shown that the soul with its functions is something distinct from matter but that it nevertheless is always accompanied by material organs and also that the soul's functions are always accompanied by organic functions which must correspond to them and that this relation is reciprocal and always will be.'

[9] *Spinoza 2. L'âme*, Paris: Aubier, p. 64: 'il s'agit là, entre les deux ordres moins d'un parallélisme que d'une identité'.

relationship between ideas and things outside thought, but also an intra-cogitative parallelism that includes two forms, depending on whether it expresses the identity between the connections of ideas and causes in the attribute of thought, or the identity of the connection of ideas taken as objects of other ideas, and the ideas of ideas.[10]

Yet, whereas the term 'parallelism' is convenient to use, insofar as it effectively conveys the idea of a correspondence between modes and attributes excluding any interaction or reciprocal causality, it is inevitably accompanied by unwelcome representations that hinder the comprehension of the unity of attributes and the union of mind and body in Spinoza. Equating the identity between the order of ideas and the order of things – and the identity between mind and body – with a system of parallel lines leads to conceptualising reality based on a model of a series of similar, matching lines that, by definition, do not intersect. Extra-cogitative parallelism thus takes the form of a multitude of lines, where the first two express the identity between the order and connection of ideas and the order and connection of bodies, the third expresses the identity between the order and the connection of ideas and of the modes of attribute X, the fourth the identity between the order and the connection of ideas and of the modes of attribute Y, and so on ad infinitum. Duplicated within the attribute of thought, the parallelism model takes on an intra-cogitative form and lines up the order and the connection of ideas and those of the idea of the idea, then the order and the connection of the ideas of the idea and those of the idea of the idea of the idea, etc.

This representation of the order of reality reduces Nature to a plane in which a plurality, or even an infinite number, of non-secant lines are juxtaposed. Yet there is a single order, as is highlighted in the Scholium to Proposition 7 of *Ethics* II: 'whether we conceive nature under the attribute of Extension, or under the attribute of Thought, or under any other attribute, we shall find the same order, *or* one and the same connection of causes, that is that the same things follow one another.' The doctrine of parallelism does not recreate the idea of unity present in Spinoza's

<hr>

[10] Ibid., p. 66ff.

system, because it introduces a form of irreducible dualism and plurality. Whereas it applies perfectly to the system in Leibniz, for whom 'the soul with its functions is something distinct from matter',[11] it would not be appropriate to explain the union as Spinoza means it. In fact, mind and body are not superimposed in humans as parallel lines, but refer to one and the same thing expressed in two ways, as the Scholium to Proposition 21 of Part II of the *Ethics* underscores. It is true that parallel lines are supposed to join in infinity, and therefore do not exclude a unifying point. We must recognise, however, that the representation of a linear series hardly recreates the unity of the individual and its composition.

Of course, it is possible to respond to this objection by asserting that the unity of parallel lines is produced by the identity of their direction. This argument, however, puts the defendants of parallelism between a rock and a hard place because it is based on a presupposition that is quite open to debate, according to which the various expressions of the same thing in each attribute go in the same direction and cannot diverge. However, this is not always true. The case of 'most errors', as analysed in the Scholium to Proposition 47 of Part II of the *Ethics*, is quite striking in this regard because it appears to be a counter-example that reveals the failures of the parallelism doctrine and largely invalidates it. Indeed, one and the same error does not express itself in the same way in the mind and body, and demonstrates a radical divergence between what happens in the mode of thought and what happens in the mode of extension. As Spinoza tells us:

Most errors consist only in our not rightly applying names to things. For when someone says that the lines drawn from the centre of a circle to its circumference are unequal, he surely understands (then at least) by a circle something different from what mathematicians understand. Similarly, when men err in calculating, they have certain numbers in their mind and different ones on the paper. So if you consider what they have in mind, they really do not err, though they seem to err because

---

[11] See 'Reflections on the Doctrine of a Single Universal Spirit' [1702], in Leroy E. Loemker (trans. and ed.), *Philosophical Papers and Letters*, p. 556.

we think they have in their mind the numbers that are on the paper. If this were not so, we would not believe that they were erring, just as I did not believe that he was erring whom I recently heard cry out that his courtyard had flown into his neighbour's hen [NS: although his words were absurd], because what he had in mind was sufficiently clear to me.[12]

While it is not possible here to analyse the full extent of Spinoza's conception of truth and falsehood, it is important to note for our analysis that the most frequent error is the disparity between what a person thinks and what he says or writes. In all the examples mentioned, the error expresses a distortion between ideas and words or, in other words, between a mode of thought and a mode of extension. Ideas, in fact, are mental phenomena, while words, whether they are uttered or put on paper, are physical phenomena. 'The essence of words and of images is constituted only by corporeal motions, which do not at all involve the concept of thought.'[13] Far from functioning in parallel, the mind and body of a mistaken person diverge profoundly. From the perspective of the mind, the error is really truth. 'If you consider what they have in Mind, they really do not err', says Spinoza. From the perspective of the body, the error is an incorrect application of names to things. The mind believes truly, but the body through its mouth or its hand expresses something else. The letter does not follow the spirit and it is this disparity that leads to the belief that people are mistaken. In reality, no one ever makes mistakes. We only conjecture that the other is mistaken, because we take his words literally and attribute them to his mind. Yet this approach is illegitimate because we transform a bodily movement into a mode of thought. In sum, we confuse the signifier with the signified. The error is only an illusion attributable to the fact that our ears do not hear sensibly what the other person's mind means intelligibly, but what his body does not transcribe identically. Spinoza concludes: 'Most controversies have arisen from this, that men do not rightly explain their own mind, or interpret the mind of the other man

---

[12] *Ethics* II, 47 Schol.; *CWS* I, 482–3.
[13] *Ethics* II, 49 Schol.; *CWS* I, 485.

badly.'[14] The necessity to interpret spoken words or text, whether sacred or profane, proves *a contrario* that the correlation between mind and body does not take on the simple form of a system of parallel lines; otherwise it would hardly be necessary to use the rules of hermeneutics to decipher meanings. A word-for-word approach would suffice to linearly bring out the meaning and move from the register of the body to that of the mind.

In this respect, the case of the slip of tongue of the man who exclaimed that 'his courtyard had flown into his neighbour's hen' is particularly revealing because the body says exactly the opposite of the mind by reversing the order of things, which is evidence indeed that parallelism is on shaky ground. The gap between body and mind is greatest here; hence their unity has nothing to do with a strict, 'twin' identity. The thought, however, is clear, and no one would have trouble understanding that the man wanted to say that the hen had flown into his neighbour's courtyard.

Does this mean, then, that the mistake is the body's and we must blame this traditional troublemaker? This question hardly makes sense inasmuch as truth or falseness are modalities of the idea and therefore fall under thought and not extension. In reality, the body is not mistaken. It expresses the same thing as the mind, but in a different register. In other words, if a bodily error occurs, it only materially signifies the truth of the mind in extension. In fact, the inversion of words relative to ideas results from a bodily movement that physically manifests agitation, surprise or confusion in the face of a heavy bird taking flight or its escape to the neighbour's. It corresponds to a state of mind and is one with it, so that the divergence in expression does not contradict psychophysical unity but reveals its full scope and complexity.

Although it seems more appropriate for expressing the correspondence between the order of adequate ideas and that of the body's affections, the parallelism doctrine remains extremely reductive and prone to misunderstandings. It presupposes homologies and one-to-one correspondences between ideas and things, mind and body, and leads to conceptualising the various modal expressions according to a linearly identical model. Except for

[14] *Ethics* II, 47 Schol.; CWS I, 482–3.

their position in space, parallel lines are similar and interchange-able. It is as if Nature were condemned to an endless echolalia, to a perpetual repetition of the same in every attribute. This doctrine leads to conceptualising unity as uniformity. Yet if the order and connection of ideas is the same as the order and connection of things, this does not necessarily mean that the modes of expres-sion of ideas and things are strictly identical and always assume the same importance. The image of the parallel system evokes the idea of a monolithic correspondence and leads to systemat-ically looking for equivalences between bodily movements and thoughts, to putting them on the same plane. Physical states are thus matched to mental states in the same way as a point on a line is connected to another point according to a strictly one-to-one model. Yet not only is such an association not always of interest, but it also does not take into account the fact that certain events are better or more strongly expressed in one register than another. In order to understand generosity, is it really necessary to describe the bodily affections that accompany this active affect in exhaus-tive detail and to dwell on its physical aspect? Conversely, is it really useful to enumerate all the muscles and cells that play a part in performing a bodily movement such as swimming? The idea of parallelism encourages attempts to translate bodily states system-atically into mental states, and vice versa. Yet even if they go hand in hand, they do not necessarily express themselves in equal terms.

Although the 'parallelism' doctrine can be illuminating in that it makes it possible to conceptualise a correspondence between mind and body without interactions or reciprocal causality, it is not really pertinent to explaining Spinoza's conception of the psychophysical union because it masks unity as well as differ-ence, and even the divergence between the modes of expression of thought and extension. Under these circumstances, all discourse on the psychophysical union comes down to the juxtaposition of two monologues that echo each other word for word, without there ever being a key phrase in one register without a matching counterpart in the other. It is therefore necessary to rethink the relationship between the idea and the object and, more generally, the relationship between the various modes of reality in Spinoza.

To do this, we must do away with 'parallelism' and get rid of this ill-fitting and ambiguous term, this muddled concept full of pitfalls that does not appear in Spinoza's system. In fact, it is not necessary to import this word, which carries along with it the surreptitious baggage of false ideas, in order to name and identify Spinoza's conception, because the author of the *Ethics* saw to it himself and provided a precise concept to express his argument known as parallelism. This concept, which a more attentive reading of the text should have brought to light long ago to avoid getting lost in the twists and turns of parallelism and its traps, is equality. This is the exact word Spinoza uses to express the fact that God's power of thinking goes hand in hand with his power of acting. The identity of the causal order in all the attributes and all the modes that depend on them is explicitly presented in the Corollary to Proposition 7 of Part II of the *Ethics*. After establishing that the order and connection of ideas is the same as that of things, Spinoza deduces from this that 'God's [NS: actual] power of thinking is *equal*[15] (*aequalis*) to his actual power of acting'. The presence of the adjective '*aequalis*' is no accident, because the author uses the same word when he compares the mind's power of thinking and the body's power of acting: 'But the Mind's striving, *or* power of thinking, is *equal*[16] to, and at one in nature with (*aequalis et simul natura*) the Body's striving, *or* power of acting.'[17] When Spinoza wants to explain that the order of the ideas of the affections in the mind corresponds to the order of the body's affections and is one and the same thing, he uses either the adjective *aequalis* or the adverb *simul*,[18] or both at once.

Consequently, whether in God or in humans, there is an equality between the power of thinking and the power of acting. In God this equality manifests itself between the attribute of thought and

---

[15] Emphasis added.

[16] Emphasis added.

[17] *Ethics* III, 28 Dem.; CWS I, 510.

[18] See *Ethics* III, 2 Schol.; CWS I, 494: 'The Mind and the Body are one and the same thing, which is conceived now under the attribute of Thought, now under the attribute of Extension. The result is that the order, *or* connection, of things is one, whether nature is conceived under this attribute or that; hence the order of actions or passions of our Body is, by nature, at one (*simul sit natura*) with the order of actions and passions of the Mind.'

the infinity of other attributes. In humans it concerns a mode of the attribute of thought, the mind, and a mode of the attribute of extension, the body. It expresses the correlation between the idea and the object and it means that 'whatever happens in the object of the idea constituting the human Mind must be perceived by the human Mind'.[19] The theory of expression in Spinoza is governed entirely by the principle of equality and must therefore be reconsidered in light of this concept.

In this respect, it is fitting to return to Gilles Deleuze's fine analyses of the parallelism doctrine in the second part of his work, *Expressionism in Philosophy: Spinoza*. Despite the precautions he takes and his avowed mistrust of the word 'parallelism',[20] Deleuze again leans on this crutch that in the end prevents him from focusing on elucidating the basic concept of equality, whose importance he has highlighted. In fact, he asserts that 'parallelism is given its strict sense by the equality of attributes, which guarantees that the connection is the same between things whose order is the same'.[21] While recognising that, contrary to Leibniz, 'Spinoza [. . .] does not use the word "parallelism",' he maintains that 'the word suits his system as he does suppose the equality of the principles from which independent and corresponding series follow'.[22] This word, however, ends up being a barrier, because it has obscured the word 'equality', which Spinoza expressly refers to, and has at times become the sanctuary of ignorance. It would therefore be more prudent to henceforth ban the term 'parallelism' and replace it with 'equality'. To be fair and accurate, we should render unto Leibniz the things that are Leibniz's . . . and unto Spinoza the things that are Spinoza's.

The Definition and Nature of Equality

Though the issue of the union of mind and body must be framed in terms of equality and not parallelism, it still remains unresolved.

[19] *Ethics* II, 12; CWS I, 502.
[20] See *Expressionism in Philosophy: Spinoza*, p. 107.
[21] Ibid., p. 108.
[22] Ibid., pp. 108–9.

We must grasp the nature of this union and specify its modalities. It is important, therefore, to pick out the occurrences of the adjective *aequalis* and the noun *aequalitas* in the system, and to find their precise meaning. The task is difficult because these terms are rare and their meaning varies from work to work. Thus, in the *Short Treatise on God, Man and His Well-Being*, Spinoza emphasises that 'there are not two equal substances' and proves this 'because every substance is perfect in its kind. For if there were two equal substances, they would necessarily have to limit one another, and consequently would not be infinite, as we have previously proven.'[23] In this context, equality expresses an identity of nature and implies the existence of a plurality of things of the same kind, which limit one another. This interpretation is corroborated by the argument developed by Spinoza in the Preface to Part II of the *Short Treatise*, which is a refusal to attribute to humanity the nature of a substance: 'Since man, then, has not existed from eternity, is limited, and equal to many men, he cannot be a substance.'[24]

It is clear that it is not in this sense of the word that Spinoza declares in the *Ethics* that 'God's [NS: actual] power of thinking is equal (*aequalis*) to his actual power of acting' because if they both express a common nature, one could not limit the other due to their infinite nature. Similarly, the equality between the mind's power of thinking and the body's power of acting cannot be understood as the expression of a reciprocal limitation because an idea can only be restricted by another idea and a body by another body.[25] This use of the adjective *aequalis* to qualify things of the same nature then disappears from the *Ethics*. Thus, in Proposition 5 of Part I, Spinoza does not demonstrate that 'there are no equal substances' but that 'in nature there cannot be two or more substances of the same nature or attribute'.

In the *Ethics*, aside from occurrences concerning the relationship between God's or humans' powers of thinking and acting, the adjective *aequo* is applied to one's frame of mind to designate its firmness, equanimity and constancy in the face of reprimands or

---

[23] *KV* I, 2.6; *CWS* I, 67.
[24] *KV* II, Praef. 3; *CWS* I, 94.
[25] See *Ethics* I, Def. 2; *CWS* I, 408.

affronts. This stands out in Chapter 13 of the Appendix to Part IV of the *Ethics*, where Spinoza mentions the case of children or teenagers who seek refuge in military service because they 'cannot bear calmly (*aequo animo*) the scolding of their parents', as well as in Chapter 14 where he states that there are more advantages than disadvantages from human society, and concludes that 'it is better to bear men's wrongs calmly (*aequo animo*)'.

This use of the term to express an equanimity of mood hardly makes it possible to elucidate the meaning of the equality between the powers of thinking and acting, unless it is his emphasis on the constancy and continuity of the power of the temperament despite variations and differences in situation. He also indicates that equanimity (*aequo animo*) involves the comparison between two different, even opposing, states and asserts itself as a power to resist and neutralise uneven moods.

Does this then mean that, in general, equality adapts to inequalities between things? In this respect it must be noted that equality in Spinoza is a relative concept that does not necessarily exclude the existence of real inequalities. It can, for example, result from an impossibility of people to perceive differences, taking into account their status of finite modes. Spinoza thus observes in Definition 6 of *Ethics* IV:

> Just as we can distinctly imagine distance of place only up to a certain limit, so also we can distinctly imagine distance of time only up to a certain limit. That is, we usually imagine all those objects which are more than 200 feet away from us, *or* whose distance from the place where we are surpasses what we can distinctly imagine, to be equally far from us; we therefore usually imagine them as if they were in the same plane; in the same way, we imagine to be equally far from the present all those objects whose time of existing we imagine to be separated from the present by an interval longer than that we are used to imagining distinctly; so we relate them, as it were, to one moment of time.

The relative nature of equality cannot be reduced to a pure illusion because the situation of things in the same space and time, when the intervals are beyond our imagination, is the positive expression of our status of finite modes and produces real effects, even if we realise our error. Spinoza thus demonstrates that our affects would be equally mild for things that are very far from the present, even though we know that they did not occur at the same time:

> From what we noted at D6, it follows that we are still affected equally mildly by objects separated from the present by an interval of time longer than we can determine by imagining, even though we may understand that they are separated from one another by a long interval of time. [26]

This form of equality, related to the suppression of inequalities resulting from an inability to imagine beyond a certain space and time, could not apply to the relationship between the powers of thinking and acting. On the one hand, it is inconceivable that God envisions equality in this manner because he does not imagine things in relation to time and space, but conceives them as they are contained in their attributes through his infinite understanding. This conclusion is also valid for a human when he stops imagining in order to conceive adequately, because his understanding is a part of God's understanding and he perceives things as actual, not in relation with a certain time and place but *sub specie aeternitatis*. Starting from the *Short Treatise*, on the other hand, Spinoza rejects the idea of any inequality between the attributes as well as between the essences of the modes: 'There is no inequality at all in the attributes, nor in the essences of the modes.'[27] We must therefore distinguish between imaginary equality resulting from the unimaginable nature of inequality, and equality that is actually conceived, which excludes an ontological inequality.

It must nevertheless be noted that the equality of power in the *Theologico-Political Treatise* is not conceptualised in the same absolute manner but, rather, relatively, depending on the yard-

---

[26] *Ethics* IV, 10 Schol.; CWS I, 552.
[27] KV App. II, 'Of the Human Mind', 11; CWS I, 154–5.

stick used as a comparison.[28] It does not imply that the things compared are identical and interchangeable, either qualitatively or quantitatively. They can be different, or even unequal, in some respects and still thought of as equal provided that this difference is negligible in other respects. Thus, it is clear that people's powers of acting and thinking are very different, depending on the various aptitudes of their bodies, and the power of the wise prevails over the ignorant. Yet, in the civil state, Spinoza tells us that 'citizens are rightly thought equal, because the power of each one is negligible compared to the power of the whole state'.[29] Similarly, the powers of thinking and acting are equal as far as the order and connection of the causes that preside over their existence are concerned, but this acknowledgement does not imply that they are in all respects equal outside the necessary correlation between the formal and objective essences.

What is more, Spinoza clearly suggests that equality cannot be confused with uniformity, but it can, on the contrary, arise from diversity and be strengthened by it. He states, in fact, in Chapter 27 of the Appendix to Part IV of the *Ethics*, that the body needs varied food and exercise to be equally capable of accomplishing everything that follows from its nature. It should not restrict itself to a repetition of the same thing; otherwise the

---

[28] This is what already stands out in the explanation Spinoza gives of Axiom IX in Part I of *The Principles of Descartes' Philosophy*, when he demonstrates the relative nature of inequality through the examples of comparing two books and two portraits: 'Suppose someone sees two books – one the work of a distinguished philosopher, the other that of some trifler, but both written in the same hand. If he attends to the meaning of the words (that is, does not attend to them insofar as they are like images), but only to the handwriting and to the order of the letters, he will recognise no inequality between them that compels him to look for different causes. They will seem to him to have proceeded from the same cause in the same way. But if he attends to the meaning of the words and the discourses, he will find a great inequality between them. And so he will conclude that the first cause of the one book was very different from the first cause of the other, and really more perfect than it in proportion to the differences he finds between the meaning of the discourses of each book, or between the words considered as images.'

[29] *TP* IX, 4; *CWS* II, 589–90.

development of its aptitudes will be unequal and will lead to over-development of some of its parts to the detriment of the whole and will be accompanied by an atrophy of the mind consumed with obsessions and stubborn affects:

> Indeed, the human Body is composed of a great many parts of different natures, which require continuous and varied food so that the whole Body may be equally capable (*aeque aptum*) of doing everything which can follow from its own nature, and consequently, so that the Mind may also be equally capable (*aeque apta*) of conceiving many things.

It appears here that the equality between the body's power of acting and the mind's power of thinking in reality demonstrates an equality of aptitudes to express all the diversity contained in each person's nature.

It is therefore important to develop research on the subject of equality and its meaning when it expresses the nature of the mind–body relationship. From this perspective, it is necessary to look into the texts of the corpus where the union of the mind and body is shown in actuality, in order to understand the diverse variations of psychophysical equality, and to shed light on its multiple facets. Part III of the *Ethics* fully satisfies these conditions, and offers a rich field of investigation insofar as it jointly analyses the mind and body's power of acting, establishing a type of discourse that simultaneously refers to thought and extension, which was not systematically the case before.

Part I, in fact, considers Nature from the perspective of its infinite attributes, and does not precisely or specifically show how a mode of thought is united to a mode of extension. Thought and extension do not play a leading role, and are only mentioned as examples.[30] Their status as attributes remains hypothetical,[31] and will only be truly established in Propositions 1 and 2 of Part II. Although it opens with the deduction of the two attributes of God we know about, Part II explains things above all on the basis of

---

[30] Cf. *Ethics* I, 21 Dem.; *CWS* I, 429–30.
[31] Cf. *Ethics* I, 14 Cor. 2; *CWS* I, 420 and I, 21 Dem.; *CWS* I, 429–30.

the attribute of thought, seeing that it aims first and foremost to determine the origin and nature of the mind, and not of humanity in general. When the body is mentioned, it is as the object of the idea constituting the mind. The only exception is the summary of physics located between Propositions 13 and 14, where things are analysed with respect to the attribute of extension.

Nevertheless, until Proposition 14, Spinoza elaborates mental and physical approaches in turn, such that discourses on the mind and body follow each other and are not systematically coordinated around a shared concept. Propositions 14 to 31, however, mark the beginning of a turning point, since they lay the groundwork for a 'mixed discourse' and provide a sampling of it through the theory of perception and imagination, which correlate an affection of the body with the idea of this affection. This mixed discourse, however, remains infrequent in Part II, and quickly gives way to the theory of knowledge and the nature of ideas, which essentially refer to the attribute of thought.

By studying the nature and origin of the affects, Part III sys-temises this new mixed approach, since it involves the union of the mind and body in actuality through the modifications that jointly concern them. It correlatively analyses the mental and bodily realities of humans with neither one preceding or proceed-ing from the other. The affects (*affectibus*), by definition, express the unity of the power of acting, since they involve a relationship with the mind as well as the body, and invite us to study them in concert. The *affectus*, for Spinoza, in fact refers to 'affections (*affectiones*) of the body by which the body's power of acting is increased or diminished, aided (*augetur*) or constrained (*coërcitur*), and at the same time (*et simul*), the ideas of these affections'.[32] Regardless of the meaning of the adverb *simul*, which we must return to later, affect covers a physical (certain affections of the body) and a mental (the ideas of these affections) reality. It holds them together and encompasses both at the same time. Affect expresses the simultaneity or contemporaneity of what happens in the mind and the body. It is not the case, in fact, that an affection of the body occurs first, which the mind then learns of by forming

---

[32] *Ethics* III, Def. 3; CWS I, 493. Translation modified.

an idea of it. It is neither the case that the mind produces physical affections, nor that the body is the cause of ideas. Any idea
of interaction or reciprocal causality is immediately ruled out.
This logical and chronological concurrence that the adverb *simul*
reveals is a consequence of the nature of the union, as Spinoza
conceptualizes it. If the mind and the body are one and the same
thing, conceived now under the attribute of thought, now under
the attribute of extension, then there necessarily must be a correlation between the two types of expression. This implies that
when Spinoza uses the future tense to describe what happens in
the mind,[33] this future does not imply the posteriority of an idea,
to come after an affection of the body, but a correspondence. It
is indicative of what we should find as an equivalent in the soul.
The affects thus appear as psychophysical realities, such that by
examining their nature and their origin, Spinoza truly promotes
a mixed discourse and breaks with the logic of 'now one, now
the other' that prevailed previously, in order to adopt the *simul*
approach.

Thus, it is by analysing the various forms of this discourse that
it will become possible to grasp more precisely the nature of the
equality between the mind and body's powers of acting and to
shed new light on the theory of expression.

---

[33] Cf. in particular *Ethics* II, 17; CWS I, 463–4: 'If the human Body is affected
with a mode that involves the nature of an external body, the human
Mind will regard (*contemplabitur*) the same external body as actually existing', and *Ethics* II, 18; CWS I, 465: 'If the human Body has once been
affected by two or more bodies at the same time, then when the Mind
subsequently imagines (*imaginabitur*) one of them, it will immediately recollect the others also.'

2

Spinoza's Break with Descartes Regarding the Affects in *Ethics* III

The Problem of the Originality of Spinoza's Conception

Despite appearances, the author of the *Ethics* is probably less inno-vative than he seems, since he was not the first to analyse the affects as joint manifestations of the mind and the body, or to have introduced a mixed discourse. In his *Letter to Elisabeth* dated 21 May 1643, Descartes had written that the passions come under the union of the soul and the body, and are explained by this 'primitive notion'.[1] The passions therefore do not depend solely on the soul or solely on the body, but on soul and body together. Indeed, they have both a physical and a mental aspect, since the soul's emotions generally involve an action of the body.[2] The Cartesian definition therefore keeps mind and body together and

---

[1] 'First I consider that there are in us certain primitive notions which are as it were the patterns on the basis of which we form all our other concep-tions. There are very few such notions. First, there are the most general – those of being, number, duration, etc. – which apply to everything we can conceive. Then, as regards body in particular, we have only the notion of extension, which entails the notions of shape and motion; and as regards the soul on its own, we have only the notion of thought, which includes the perceptions of the intellect and the inclinations of the will. Lastly, as regards the soul and the body together, we have only the notion of their union, on which depends our notion of the soul's power to move the body, and the body.' *AT* III, p. 665.

[2] Cf. *Passions of the Soul* I, II.

involves both at once. Passion is a physical reality as regards its cause and a mental one as regards its effects. That is why it is not explained by the primitive notion of thought or by the primitive notion of extension, but only on the basis of the union. Yet the union implies that we conceive of soul and body as one thing. This is what emerges from Descartes' *Letter to Elisabeth* of 28 June 1643, in which he maintains that 'to conceive of the union between two things is to conceive of them as one single thing'.[3] After meditating on the factors that prove the distinction between soul and body, he invites his correspondent 'to represent to herself the notion of the union that each always experiences within himself without philosophising, in knowing that he is a single person who has together a body and a thought.'[4] The authorship of the third discourse of ontological identity therefore belongs to Descartes, who tries to go beyond the dualism of substances to conceptualise a human being in his unity. Yet, among the derived notions that allow us to re-examine this union are the voluntary actions of the soul on the body and the passions.

The concept of passion plays a key role in the Cartesian system, since it demonstrates this union operating under the influence of the institution of nature, and allows us to shed light on its incomprehensible essence. The *Letters to Elisabeth* and the *Passions of the Soul* develop a mixed discourse, as Paul Ricoeur rightly asserts.[5] In his last work, Descartes begins by examining the difference between the soul and the body in order to determine their respective functions, and then returns to them in their unity. The first part of the *Passions of the Soul* thus combines three approaches: a purely physical approach, in Articles VII to XVI where Descartes analyses our body as a machine; a mental approach in Articles XVII to XXIX where the functions of the soul are defined; and, finally, a psychophysical approach in Articles XXX to L where the union is conceptualised, in turn, as an interaction[6] or in the form

---

[3] AT III, p. 692.
[4] AT III, pp. 693–4.
[5] Cf. *What Makes Us Think?* p. 33.
[6] Cf. Article XXXIV: 'How the soul and the body act on each other.'

of a 'parallelism'[7] between the soul's inclinations and the body's movements. From this perspective, Spinoza's approach is analogous to Descartes': in the *Ethics* he successively adopts a physical approach by briefly laying out the premises concerning the body after Proposition 13 of Part II, then a mental approach by analysing the nature and origin of the mind, in order to then re-examine them together through the affects.

Against this background, one may wonder what is so special and original about Spinoza's definition of the affects, since already in Descartes passion is a psychophysical reality. It would be useless to assert that the concept of affect is broader than that of the passions, seeing that it also covers actions. Descartes, in fact, also accepts the idea of an active affectivity to a certain extent, since he distinguishes two types of emotion: 'internal emotions which are produced in the soul only by the soul itself'[8] and passive emotions caused by the body. The internal, or intellectual, emotions simultaneously involve an action and a passion of the soul, since the soul is both the agent that causes them and the recipient that experiences them. But, if according to Article XIX of the *Passions of the Soul*, 'names are always determined by whatever is most noble', internal emotions can legitimately be called actions.[9]

It is therefore crucial to determine how Spinoza differentiates himself from Descartes. The question is not purely an academic one, since Spinoza positions himself explicitly with respect to the Cartesian frame of reference. Indeed, Descartes is the only author Spinoza specifically mentions when he presents his theory of the affects and whom he takes the trouble to refute at length in the Preface to Part V.[10] That is why it is necessary to examine

---

[7] Cf. Article XL: 'What the principal effect of the passions is': 'The principal effect of all the human passions is that they move and dispose the soul to want the things for which they prepare their body.'

[8] *Passions of the Soul* II, CXLVII.

[9] On the relationship between Cartesian interior emotions and Spinoza's active affects, see Jean-Marie Beyssade's article, 'De l'émotion intérieure chez Descartes à l'affect actif spinoziste', in E. Curley and P.-F. Moreau (eds), *Spinoza: Issues and Directions* (Leiden: Brill, 1990), pp. 176–90.

[10] Jean-Marie Beyssade observes for that matter that 'Spinoza in the entire *Ethics* only cites one author, Descartes, and only one book by this author,

how Spinoza situates himself with respect to Descartes, as well as distancing himself from the French philosopher, starting from the Preface to *Ethics* III, in order to understand the specificity of his conception and shed light on the nature of the mixed discourse that correlates the soul and body through the concept of affect.

In the Preface, Spinoza announces his intention to take a fresh look at the origin and nature of the affects and distinguishes himself from his predecessors who, by his own admission, have all failed in this undertaking. He deals with Descartes separately, however, and initiates an odd break with the author of the *Passions of the Soul*:

> But no one, to my knowledge, has determined the nature and powers of the affects, nor what, on the other hand, the mind can do to moderate them. I know, of course, that the celebrated Descartes, although he too believed that the mind has abso-lute power over its own actions, nevertheless sought to explain human affects through their first causes, and at the same time to show the way by which the mind can have absolute dominion over its affects. But in my opinion, he showed nothing but the cleverness of his understanding, as I shall show in the proper place.[11]

It is truly an odd break because, first of all, it takes the form of a tribute that gets turned on its head, as if Descartes' strengths were really his weaknesses: 'He showed nothing but the cleverness of his understanding (*magni sui ingenii acumen ostendit*).' Descartes is certainly shrewd, but that is all he is. What does this mean? This comment, which may appear at first glance to be ironic or purely rhetorical, is in reality neither fortuitous nor accidental, since Spinoza reiterates it in the Preface to *Ethics* V, where he presents Descartes' opinion on the soul's absolute power over the passions and confesses that he 'would hardly have believed it had been

the *Passions of the Soul* (III, Praef.; V, Praef).' Cf. 'De l'émotion intérieure chez Descartes à l'affect actif spinoziste', in E. Curley and P.-F. Moreau (eds), *Spinoza: Issues and Directions* (Leiden: Brill, 1990), p. 177.

[11] *Ethics* III, Praef.; CWS I, 491–2.

propounded by so great a man, had it not been so subtle (*si minus acuta fuisset*)'. The question, then, is to find out where Descartes is shrewd, and where his acuity is at the same time an admission of his failure to understand the nature of the affects and the means to govern them. What does this shrewdness that is both laudatory and derogatory mean, exactly?

It is a curious break, second of all, because it was postponed almost as soon as it was announced. Spinoza maintains that he will prove the argument he is putting forward in the proper place (*ut suo loco*) and, in fact, the critique in due form of Descartes' theories only appears in the Preface to Part V of the *Ethics*. For the time being, Spinoza leaves Descartes aside and proposes 'to return to those who prefer to curse or laugh at the Affects and actions of men, rather than understand them'.[12] So it is as if this critique had no place here and must be put off so as not to appear misplaced. Under these circumstances, we can ask ourselves why Spinoza mentions Descartes here, while deferring his critique until Part V – in sum, making room for something that had no place there. Is it not strange to announce a sensational break in Part III and only complete it in Part V?

The Tribute to Descartes' *Ingenium*

To understand the nature of the critique and its provisional post-ponement, we need, first, to elucidate this ambiguous praise and define the perspicacity attributed to Descartes' intelligence. To this end, we must note that Spinoza does not praise Descartes for the power of his intellect (*intellectus*) but for the acuity of his *ingenium*, a term generally translated in English as 'genius' or 'intelligence', and that in Spinoza generally refers to the idea of temperament or the constitution of beings. The *ingenium* is a concept that applies not only to an individual but also to a people, a nation, the vulgar or the crowd.[13] The *ingenium* refers to the lasting characteristics related to thinking habits, lifestyle and history, which make an individual or people recognisable

---

[12] *Ethics* III, Praef.; CWS I, 491–2.
[13] Cf. *TTP* III, 43; CWS II, 121, IV, 17; CWS II, 129; V, 44; CWS II, 150.

by distinguishing them from others.[14] The *ingenium* can manifest itself as a very lively imagination, as in the case of prophets, and as reason, as in the case of the free man. In the free man, indeed, the *ingenium* is associated with a rational manner of living, as the Scholium to Proposition 64 of *Ethics* IV demonstrates, where Spinoza uses the expression '*ingenio et vivendi ratione pauca*' about the free man. As for the Cartesian *ingenium*, it is characterised neither by imagination, like the prophet's, nor by reason, like the free man's, but rather by its acuity.

Based on an examination of its textual occurrences, *acutus* is an adjective Spinoza uses to qualify beings with insight into human affairs, who understand human nature and how to govern people. Apart from Descartes, Spinoza applies this qualifier to:

- politicians who use their experience to establish laws that are well suited to humankind. He also maintains in the *Political Treatise*[15] that 'the men who discussed and established the common laws and public affairs were very acute (*vires acutissimis*) (whether cunning or shrewd)'.
- Machiavelli, on two occasions in the *Political Treatise* in Chapter V.7: 'Machiavelli, ever shrewd (*acutissimus Machiavellus prolixe ostendit*), has shown in detail the means a Prince must use to stabilise and preserve his rule, if all he craves is to be master'; in Chapter X.1: 'The primary cause for the dissolution of states of this kind is the one that most acute Florentine noted (*acutissimus florentinus observat*) in Bk. III, Disc. i of his *Discourses on Titus Livy*.' Machiavelli is called acute on the subject of the preservation of states, on the one hand, and their disintegration, on the other. This acuity refers rather to a practical intelligence based on observation and experience. Machiavelli does not prove his remarks with geometrical reasons; instead, he shows (*ostendit*) and observes (*observat*).

---

[14] On the concept of the *ingenium*, see Pierre-François Moreau, *L'expérience et l'éternité*, II, III, p. 379ff.

[15] *TP* I, 3; CWS II, 504–5.

Does this mean, then, that Descartes' *ingenium*, like Machiavelli's, is characterised by a certain form of practical wisdom and prudence that leads one to take experience into account and dispense useful advice to people? Certain clues may lead us to think that is indeed the case, since Spinoza, although by and large critical of the failure of his predecessors to found a science of affects and their mastery, does not put them all in the same basket. He recognises eminent individuals, to whom he admits owing a great deal, who 'have written many admirable things about the right way of living, and given men advice full of prudence'.[16] Yet, immediately after this comment, he mentions Descartes as if he were part of this category. Nonetheless, in the same way that Machiavelli is not a simple empiricist whose reflections can be reduced to a collection of observations and recipes to manipulate people, it does not appear that Descartes is reduced to these distinguished men, educated by the lessons of experience. The Machiavellian model goes well beyond that, and invites us to conceptualise acuity not only as a form of practical knowledge but also as a new manner of speculating that is both reasonable and well reasoned.

Machiavelli demonstrates great acuity, since he belongs neither to the category of daydreaming philosophers who devise utopias where people will live in perpetual perfect harmony, nor to that of melancholy philosophers who satirise human vices. He applies himself to identifying the principles and rules of political action based on people as they are and not on how they should be. In doing this, he lays the foundations of a rigorous political science.

The same applies to Descartes, who does not seek to put the passions and human nature on trial, but rather to discover the mechanisms governing them. He demonstrates acuity since he 'sought to explain human Affects through their first causes, and at the same time to show the way by which the Mind can have absolute dominion over its Affects'.[17] Indeed, in a letter to Father Picot dated 14 August 1649, Descartes confesses his intention to develop a science of the passions: 'My intention was to explain

---

[16] *Ethics* III Praef.; CWS I, 491–2.
[17] *Ethics* III, Praef.; CWS I, 491–2.

the passions only as a natural philosopher [*physicien*], and not as a rhetorician or even a moral philosopher.' He adopts a dispassionate attitude with respect to the passions and considers them to be natural objects of study. Descartes is astute because, deep down, he is the first Spinozist.

Descartes was ahead of his time in that he applied the precept that governs Spinoza's approach in *Ethics* III. He refuses to mock the passions, hate them or hold them in contempt. Instead, he applies himself to understanding them. He therefore demonstrates wisdom that goes beyond his predecessors', since he tries to find out the principles governing emotions and considers control of the passions secondary to knowledge of their causes. He has the same aim as the author of the *Ethics*, namely to develop a science of the passions and to define the power of the mind in order to master them. The approaches taken by these two philosophers are somewhat analogous, so that, in many respects, Spinoza remains in the Cartesian school.

First, in both Spinoza and Descartes, the analysis begins by calling into question previous works on the subject. In Article I of the *Passions of the Soul*, Descartes observes that 'the defects of the sciences we have from the ancients are nowhere more apparent than in their writings on the passions'. It is the same assessment of failure that opens the Preface to *Ethics* III. More specifically, Descartes dismisses two approaches: the rhetoricians' and the moral philosophers'.

First, he refuses to deal with the passions as a rhetorician, and thus breaks with the Jesuit tradition that recommends using literature for teaching morality. Based on readings of Latin poets and philosophers such as Seneca and Cicero, this approach was more rhetorical than scientific, since it aimed to describe the passions in the most touching way possible in order to urge the audience to fight against some passions and practise others. It was therefore more a question of talking about the passions for cathartic ends than shedding light on their nature and laws.

Descartes also refused to deal with the passions as a moral philosopher. He thus distanced himself from Thomas Aquinas and the Scholastics, who explained the passions from an ethical perspective and subsumed them under moral philosophy. In the

Summa Theologica, Aquinas' starting point is the beatitude of the soul; then he analyses its actions and finally its passions. Descartes also distances himself from moralists such as Bodin, Montaigne and Charron, who see the passions falling under morality rather than science, since they do not obey constant laws. In fact, the moral philosophers conceptualised the passions as disruptions, violent movements that disturb the soul and are more like the meteors of physics than regular, everyday phenomena. Therefore, mastering the passions falls more under the category of wisdom or the art of living than science.

Spinoza, in turn, dismisses all approaches similar to the two Cartesian categories – rhetoricians and moral philosophers – although he does not overlap with them exactly. Indeed, he distinguishes himself from what one could call the moralists 'who prefer to curse or laugh at the Affects and actions of men, rather than understand them'.[18] In this section, Spinoza includes three figures that he later makes explicit in the Scholium to Proposition 35 of *Ethics* V, namely theologians who curse the actions of humankind, the satirists who scoff at them and the melancholics who disdain them. Spinoza, like Descartes, rejects the moral philosophers who believe that mankind disrupts the natural order rather than following it and who denounce human vices. He also critiques in his own way the rhetoricians who satirise the passions and vilify human nature: 'He who knows how to censure more eloquently and cunningly the weakness of the human Mind is held to be Godly.'[19]

Second, their methods of investigation have an undeniable similarity despite having different names. Although the passions of the soul bring into play the union and are in reality of a psychophysical nature, Descartes seeks to explain them as a natural philosopher [*physicien*]. What does this mean? Physics, according to the preface of *Principles of Philosophy*, is the science of nature as a whole and it determines the true principles of material things. It includes three main parts: a general examination of how the universe is composed, a more specific study of the earth and all

18 Ibid.
19 Ibid.

the bodies and, finally, knowledge of the nature of plants, animals and humankind.[20] Dealing with the passions as a natural philosopher means, first of all, recognising that they are an integral part of nature and subject to laws that can be known clearly and distinctly. The passions of the soul, for Descartes, in one sense, are not the soul's passions. Rather, they are passions in the soul but do not stem from it. There are therefore perceptions that are determined by something other than the soul alone. Descartes then applies himself to seeking the causes that act upon the soul in passion. The passions have a physical cause, the action of the body. That is why he must explain them as a natural philosopher by demonstrating the bodily mechanism operating in them. Descartes reintegrates the passions into human nature without railing against them. They are not bad in themselves and they have a place within the institution of nature. They play a decisive role in the preservation of the union of soul and body. Indeed, passions incite the soul to want the things for which they prepare the body. They therefore have a function which

> consists solely in this: that they dispose our soul to want the things which nature deems useful for us, and to persist in this volition; and the same agitation of the spirits which normally causes the passions also disposes the body to make movements which help us attain these things'.[21]

Descartes later says, for that matter, that 'they are all by nature good, and that we have nothing to avoid but their misuse or their excess'.[22]

Spinoza also calls for this naturalisation and rationalisation of the passional phenomenon when he proposes to deal with them geometrically. This approach involves breaking with those who considered the passions as things outside nature and contrary to

---

[20] Cf. *Principles of Philosophy*, Preface, AT IX, p. 14.

[21] *The Passions of the Soul* II LII.

[22] *The Passions of the Soul* III CCXI. This judgement is more nuanced in Descartes' letter to Chanut dated 1 November 1646: 'In examining the passions I have found almost all of them to be good.' AT IV, p. 538.

reason. Although he does not share the idea that the passions have a purpose in the institution of nature, he does not disown Descartes when it comes to postulating a causal order behind the apparent disorder of the passions. Like him, he accepts the principle of an enumeration and a deduction of complex affects from primitive affects, although he does not agree with him on the number and nature of the said affects. Admittedly, Descartes proposes to explain the passions as a natural philosopher, while Spinoza positions himself as a geometrician who considers 'human actions and appetites just as if it were a Question of lines, planes and bodies'.[23] However, the different name of the method does not indicate a divergence of principle, since the geometric model is not in contradiction with the physical model. It must be noted that Spinoza also deals with the affects as a natural philosopher, to the extent that he contemplates considering them as bodies. This is even more evident in his *Political Treatise*, where he maintains having taken

> great pains not to laugh at human actions, or mourn them, or curse them, but only to understand them. So I've contemplated human affects – like love, hate, anger, envy, love of esteem, compassion and the other emotions – not as vices of human nature, but as properties which pertain to it in the same way heat, cold, storms, thunder, etc., pertain to the nature of the air.[24]

Finally, when we know that physics in Descartes is of a geometric nature and boils down to the science of the extended substance in length and depth, it becomes clear that both authors are seeking to construct a geometry of the passions in several dimensions.

In both cases the geometric model is at work and, more specifically, the linear model. From that perspective, Descartes and Spinoza borrow the way they formulate and solve problems from the ancient geometers. For Descartes, the means of knowing things relates first and foremost to lines: 'In order the better to

---

[23] *Ethics* III Praef.; CWS I, 491–2.
[24] TP I.4; CWS II, 505.

consider them separately I should suppose them to hold between lines', he wrote in the second part of his *Discourse on the Method*.[25] Spinoza also invites us to consider human appetites as if it were a question of lines. This model is based on that of the ancient geometers, who made use of lines to solve problems. They even went as far as naming the problems according to the type of line they required. This is what Pappus of Alexandria reported in the third century in his collection, which brings together a large part of the works of Greek geometers and was translated in 1588:

> The ancients stated that there are three kinds of geometrical problem, and that some are called plane, others solid and others line-like; and those that can be solved by straight lines and the circumference of a circle are rightly called plane because the lines by means of which these problems are solved have their origin in the plane. But such problems that must be solved by assuming one or more conic sections in the construction are called solid because for their construction it is necessary to use the surfaces of solid figures, namely cones. There remains a third kind that is called line-like. For in their construction other lines than the ones just mentioned are assumed, having an inconstant and changeable origin, such as spirals and the curves that the Greeks call *tetragonizousas* ['square-making'], and which we call 'quandrantes' and conchoids and cissoids, which have many amazing properties.[26]

Descartes explicitly mentions this classification in his *Geometry* at the beginning of Book II,[27] and although he objects to some of the confusion in naming lines and in their degrees of composition, he accepts the idea that all geometry problems can be reduced to the construction of lines.[28] Although Spinoza does not directly

[25] Cf. AT VI, p. 20.
[26] Pappus (1876–8), *Collectionis quae supersunt*, ed. F. Hultsch (Berlin: Waldman), III, 7. Eng. trans. by H. J. M. Bos, in *Redefining Geometrical Exactness: Descartes' Transformation of the Early Modern Concept of Construction* (New York: Springer, 2001), p. 38.
[27] Cf. AT VI, p. 388.
[28] Cf. *Geometry*, Book I, AT VI, p. 369 (2): 'All the problems of geometry can

refer in the *Ethics* to the methods of the ancient geometers inventoried by Pappus, it is not inconceivable to also see a trace of this model of problem solving in the reference to lines, planes and bodies. The entire geometry of affects, as complex as they may be, can always be simplified to the first dimension, since everything can be explained and deduced on the basis of the three primary affects. Desire, joy and sadness[29] are similar to lines that allow us to construct all the affects without exception. Love and hate, as they involve the composition of joy and sadness with the idea of an external cause, lead us to the second dimension and coincide with planes. However, the question of whether the analogy can be maintained to the end is a delicate one, since it is more difficult to identify with certainty the affects that would correspond to bodies and to the third dimension.[30] In any event, it is clear that the plan to establish a science of the passions is common to both authors, so that Descartes can be thought of as Spinoza's precursor.

That is why we must pay tribute to his astute mind. Not only did Descartes break with the common attitude that made passion an irrational phenomenon against nature, but he also formulated the problem in terms that made it possible to find a solution. Rigorous knowledge of the principles and laws governing the passions is indeed a precondition for control over them. What makes Descartes an astute philosopher is that he applied himself to determining the primary causes of the passions, subordinating the issue of their mastery to this investigation.

We still have to understand why he did not demonstrate anything other than his cleverness. Spinoza is elliptical on this subject

---

easily be reduced to such terms that thereafter we need to know only the length of certain strait lines in order to construct them.'

[29] Cf. *Ethics* III, 11 Schol.; *CWS* I, 500–1.

[30] Some commentators, such as Pierre Macherey (Cf. *Introduction à l'Ethique de Spinoza, La troisième partie*, p. 184.), consider that the imitation of the affects, in *Ethics* III, 21, is the beginning of a new stage. It is true that it is a decisive turning point involving interpersonal relationships, but there is nothing to literally confirm that it represents the third dimension and a counterpart to bodies and solids. For that matter, there is no reason to stop at the third dimension, since the combination of affects can continue indefinitely and become more and more complex.

in *Ethics* III, but he suggests that, although Descartes rose above his predecessors, he did not manage to avoid the same pitfalls, since no one to his knowledge was able to determine the true nature of the affects and the power of the mind over them. In short, the author of the *Passions of the Soul* framed the problem well but was unable to solve it. He demonstrated acuity because he cleared the way, but in the end he committed himself to a dead end. At present, we must explain their fundamental differences of opinion and why the announced critique is postponed until Part V of the *Ethics*.

The Reasons for the Break

The break is mainly about the two points already stated in the Preface to *Ethics* III, namely the nature of the cause of the passions and the nature of the power of the mind over them. Although Spinoza and Descartes agree that the passions have a natural *raison d'être*, they diverge radically on their primary causes. For Descartes, passions in the general sense are perceptions of the soul that can have two causes: the soul and the body.[31] The perceptions that have the soul as their cause are those of our volitions, our imaginings or the thoughts that depend on them. In one sense they are passions, since the soul cannot prevent itself from perceiving that it is willing something at the very moment that it is doing so: 'Although willing something is an action with respect to our soul, the perception of such willing may be said to be a passion in the soul.'[32] However, for Descartes, since the perception of willing and the willing itself are but one and the same thing, it is possible to consider it to be an action of the soul. The passions of the soul, having the soul as their cause, can legitimately be called actions of the soul. They are not passions in the strictest sense, seeing that the soul is both the agent and the recipient. For Descartes, 'the names are always determined by whatever is most noble; we do not call it a 'passion' but solely an 'action'.[33]

[31] Cf. *Passions of the Soul* I, XIX.
[32] Ibid.
[33] Ibid.

Passions, in the strict sense of the term, have an action of the body as their cause.[34] Descartes, in fact, accepts a correlation between action and passion. Actions and passions are different names for the same change. Passion refers to the change from the point of view of the subject who experiences it, of the recipient who is moved and touched. Action indicates the change from the point of view of the subject who makes it happen, the agent who moves and touches. The passion of the soul is an action of the body; it is a physical reality as regards its cause, which allows us to understand why, in the final analysis, Descartes tries to explain the passions as a natural philosopher. Passions entail understanding the body's functions and movements. In the most precise and determined sense, the passions of the soul are caused by the movement of animal spirits, the small particles in the blood filtered by the brain that move very quickly and mechanically continue their motion in a closed circuit. In Article XXVII, Descartes describes passions very precisely as 'perceptions, sensations or emotions of the soul which we refer particularly to it, and which are caused, maintained and strengthened by some movement of the spirits'.

It is at the end of the definition where the two authors diverge. This already stands out in the Preface to *Ethics* III, where Spinoza observes that among all those who had written about the affects, no one had determined their nature and cause. This is also confirmed by the small comment inserted into the quotation of the Cartesian definition in the Preface to *Ethics* V. Spinoza wholly accepts the first part, according to which the passions are 'perceptions, sensations or emotions of the soul which we refer particularly to it', but he draws attention to the cause that Descartes attributes to them with a *Nota bene*.[35] For him, the proximate cause of the passions could not be the movement of animal spirits. In fact, Spinoza distinguishes two types of affects depending on their productive cause: actions and passions. It is, for that matter, one of the reasons why he starts from the more general concept of affect that covers both actions and passions. Actions are affects of which we are the adequate, or complete, cause – in other words, those that

---

[34] Cf. *Passions of the Soul* I, 2.
[35] *Ethics* V Pref.; CWS I, 594–7.

are explained only by our nature. Passions, on the other hand, are affects of which we are an inadequate, or partial, cause, namely those that are not explained solely by our nature but that also involve external causes.

It is possible that Spinoza would agree with Descartes in saying that actions depend only on the mind, but in no case would he accept the idea that the passions are caused by the body. For him, the passive affects cover, like any affect, a physical and corporeal reality, since they are constituted at the same time (*simul*) by the affections of the body and by the idea of these affects, but the cause of passion is to be sought somewhere other than in the body. Mind and body are one and the same thing, explained in two ways with respect to either extension or thought. They do not interact with each other; rather, they act and are acted upon in concert. For Spinoza, 'the Body cannot determine the Mind to thinking, and the Mind cannot determine the Body to motion, to rest, or to anything else (if there is anything else)'.[36] The passions therefore do not depend on the body but on inadequate ideas, while actions arise from adequate ideas. Explaining passions is not about understanding the actions of the body but understanding the formation of inadequate ideas. In fact, it involves explaining why the mind is not always a complete or adequate cause of its ideas, why it is sometimes a partial cause or inadequate cause of its idea, and hence acted upon. The reason stems from the place a human being occupies within nature and his ontological status of a finite mode that cannot avoid being subjected to changes of which he is not the adequate cause. A human being is only a part of nature, which cannot be conceived through itself without the other parts.[37] The changes that affect a human therefore cannot always be explained solely by the laws of his nature.[38] The human is subject to the action of external causes, which do not necessarily suit his nature, and is acted upon by them.

This first divergence regarding the cause of the passions leads to a second one about how the soul can moderate and acquire con-

---

[36] *Ethics* III, 2; CWS I, 494.
[37] Cf. *Ethics* IV, 2; CWS I, 548.
[38] Cf. *Ethics* IV, 4; CWS I, 548.

trol over them. Like a good number of authors who have written about the affects, Descartes 'too believed that the mind has absolute power over its own actions'.[39]

Indeed, for Descartes, the soul, by virtue of its free will and infinite volition, has an absolute and direct power over its actions. Admittedly, it has only indirect and relative influence over its passions[40] since, once they are unleashed following a movement of the animal spirits, the soul cannot have the passions entirely at its command. Passion is an action of the body and remains present in our thought as long as the movement in the heart, blood and spirits has not stopped.[41] Although the soul is endowed with absolute power over its actions and volitions, it does not immediately have it over its passions. It can easily overcome weak passions, such as hearing a slight noise or feeling a slight pain, by creating a distraction or by paying attention to something else, but it cannot surmount strong ones 'except after the disturbance of the blood and spirits has died down'.[42] On this subject, Descartes explains that

> the most the will can do while this disturbance is at full strength is not to yield to its effects and to inhibit many of the movements to which it disposes the body. For example, if anger causes the hand to rise to strike a blow, the will can usually restrain it; if fear moves the legs in flight, the will can stop them; and similarly in other cases.[43]

Although the soul has only an indirect power over the body, once passion has been set in motion, it can achieve absolute mastery of its emotions. This is what Article L highlights by showing that 'there is no soul so weak that it cannot, if well directed, acquire absolute power over its passions'. How is this possible? The interaction between the soul and body, in Descartes, occurs via the pineal gland, located at the back of the brain, in such a

[39] *Ethics* III Pref.; CWS I, 491–2.
[40] *Passions of the Soul* I, XLI.
[41] *Passions of the Soul* I, XLVI.
[42] Ibid.
[43] Ibid.

way that every movement of the gland is joined to a thought. This correspondence between a movement of the gland and a thought is an institution of nature, so that fear in the soul disposes the body to make a movement of flight. But it can also be modified by habit and effort so that anger, for example, which is naturally accompanied by a movement of the gland that pushes a great deal of animal spirits into the arms to strike, is associated with another movement, such as restraint. Exercise and training, examples of which are given in Article L, can thus modify the course of the animal spirits and allow one to acquire absolute power over the passions. Whether innate or acquired, in Descartes there is thus an absolute power of the soul, not only over its actions, but also over its passions. This dominion of the soul is in reality control over the body, whether it is in the case of voluntary movement or of mastering the passions through exercise and habit.

Spinoza might possibly concede to Descartes that the soul has absolute power over its actions, if by 'absolute power' we do not mean that which falls under free will but that which draws its determination only from itself. Indeed, the active affects are explained only by our nature and depend only on the power of the mind or the body, which amounts to the same thing. He might also agree with the author of the *Passions of the Soul* that the well-directed soul can gain control over its passions. On the other hand, this control is never control over the body and it could never be absolute, as the Preface to *Ethics* V reminds us, even though this part of the work is devoted to the freedom and the power of the intellect.[44] The dominion is not a dominion of the soul over the body but of the soul over itself. The key to the explanation of the passions and the power of the soul over them lies in exact knowledge of the power of the mind, in determining what it can and cannot do. It is not possible for there to be no passions, as Proposition 4 of *Ethics* V and its corollary show:

It is impossible that a man should not be a part of Nature, and that he should be able to undergo no changes except those

---

[44] *Ethics* V, Praef.; CWS I, 595: 'For we have already demonstrated above that it does not have an absolute dominion over them (the affects).'

which can be understood through his own nature alone, and of which he is the adequate cause [. . .] From this it follows that man is necessarily always subject to passions, that he follows and obeys the common order of Nature, and accommodates himself to it as much as the nature of things requires.

It is possible to ensure that any passive affect ceases to exist, thanks to the power of understanding: 'An affect which is a passion ceases to be a passion as soon as we form a clear and distinct idea of it.'[45] This is valid for all affects since 'there is no affection of the Body of which we cannot form a clear and distinct concept'.[46] The wise person, consequently, is not exempt from the passions but can make them cease as soon as they begin. It is the dominion of knowledge that protects mankind from the dominion of the common order of nature. Everything therefore stems from the power of understanding. In other words, for Spinoza, knowing the cause of the passions and determining the remedy or the means to contain them are not two separate questions. They lead back to one and the same thing, namely acquiring exact knowledge of the power of the mind, to a confrontation between human nature and nature as a whole.

In reality, Spinoza reproaches Descartes for being ignorant of the power of the mind and its true nature. If Descartes gets the cause of the passions wrong, it is because he believes that the body can affect the mind. An action of the body on the soul is indeed only possible if we accept that the soul has a nature such that it can be subject to the movements of a mode of extension. If Descartes gets the remedy to the passions wrong by attributing to the soul the power of acting back on the body, and of acquiring an absolute power over the passions by being well directed, it is because he believes that we can voluntarily join the body's movements to the soul's firm and determined judgements. Descartes does not know what the mind is capable of, and all his errors regarding the causes of and the remedy to the passions stem from this. We can thus understand why Spinoza, in the Preface to Part III, postpones his

[45] Cf. Ethics V, 3; CWS I, 598.
[46] Ethics V, 4; CWS I, 598.

explanation of why Descartes only demonstrated insightfulness. To remedy Descartes' errors it is important to have an adequate idea of the nature and limits of the power of the mind, which serve as a standard and make it possible to separate truth from falsehood. That is why the critique of Descartes' theory could only occur in Part V, which is expressly devoted to the power of the intellect and human freedom. There was no reason for it earlier, unless it was simply to announce what lay in store for the reader. Once the causes of the passions and servitude were determined in Part IV and the causes of actions and freedom in Part V, the error would disappear on its own and the Cartesian conception would reveal itself for what it is: an 'occult' hypothesis, a fiction.

After being deferred, a proper demonstration of Descartes' errors can then take place, centred around four main points:

1. The critique of the fiction of the union of the soul and body, and the location of the seat of the soul in the pineal gland. The soul as a thinking substance cannot be united to a small part of matter.
2. The critique of the fiction of the interaction between the forces of the soul and the body's movements, which, by virtue of their heterogeneous nature, are not commensurate.
3. The critique of the fiction of the pineal gland.
4. The critique of the fiction of a free will and an absolute power.

When all is said and done, if Machiavelli is very shrewd because he was able to determine how a prince can preserve his dominion, Descartes is merely somewhat shrewd because he was not able to determine how the soul could preserve its own dominion. He grasped the problem but did not go further. In short, all his astuteness can be summed up as having given false solutions to true problems.

3

The Different Origins of the Affects in the Preface to the *Theological-Political Treatise* and in the *Ethics*

The Reasons for the Comparison

Although Spinoza breaks completely with Descartes in order to found a new science of the affects in the Preface to *Ethics* III, the fact remains that the author of the *Passions of the Soul* left a mark on the former's youthful works. Indeed, in the *Short Treatise*, the analysis of the nature of the affects still embraces a Cartesian model on at least two levels.

First, the nature of the causality that governs the relationship between the soul and the body remains in part Cartesian. Admittedly, Spinoza distances himself from Descartes by refusing to accept that the body is the principal cause of the passions of the soul. The proximate cause of the affects (*lijdingen*) in the soul is knowledge – in other words, a mode of thinking. Affects can only be experienced by a being who conceives and who is constituted by modes of thinking. Thus love, desire, and all of the affects in general stem from three different modes of knowledge by which humans understand themselves: opinion (*waan*), which is based on a conception through hearsay and experience; true belief (*geloof*), which involves apprehending things and their necessity through reason without direct vision; and clear knowledge (*klaare kennisse*), which does not come from being convinced by reasons but from the awareness and enjoyment of the thing itself.[1] All affects and passions, such as hate and aversion, that are contrary

[1] *KV* II, 2, 2; *CWS* I, 98–9.

to right reason come from opinion. All affects or passions that are good desires, such as legitimate self-satisfaction and humility, which encompass knowing one's perfection according to its true worth, arise from belief.[2] Finally, clear knowledge produces pure, true love, namely the love of God.

Although all affects are the product of a mode of knowledge, Spinoza nevertheless continues to accept the idea of reciprocal action of the soul on the body and vice versa. In the *Short Treatise*, Spinoza is therefore partly subject to the very critiques he would later elaborate in Part III of the *Ethics*, since he contemplates the possibility of an interaction between the soul and the body and one producing an effect on the other.[3] These effects are admittedly limited, but real. Although the soul is never the cause of the body's movement or rest, it nevertheless has the power to move the animal spirits and to change their direction.[4] Though it cannot explain what happens to the soul, the body is the cause of the soul's perception of it.[5]

In the *Ethics*, no trace of these conceptions remains. The modifications of movement, when they are compelled, are presented as aptitudes of the body without identifying the agent that determines them.[6] It appears, however, to be out of the question for the soul to

[2] *KV* II, 8, 3; *CWS* I, 111.

[3] *KV* II, 19, 11–14; *CWS* I, 132–3.

[4] *KV* II, 19, 11; *CWS* I, 132–3: 'The soul [acting] on the body, as we have already said, can bring it about that the spirits which would otherwise have moved in one direction, should now, however, move in another.'

[5] *KV* II, 19, 13; *CWS* I, 133: 'Having said this much about the actions of the soul on the body, let us now examine the actions of the body on the soul. We maintain that the principal one is that it causes the soul to perceive it, and thereby to perceive other bodies also. This is caused only by Motion and Rest together. For there are no other things in the body through which it could act.'

[6] Cf. *Ethics* II, 13 Lem. 6; *CWS* I, 461: 'If certain bodies composing an Individual are compelled to alter the motion they have from one direction to another, but so that they can continue their motions and communicate them to each other in the same ratio as before, the individual will likewise retain its nature, without any change of form,' and Lem. 7; *CWS* I, 461: 'Furthermore, the Individual so composed retains its nature, whether it, as a whole, moves or is at rest, or whether it moves in this or that direction, so long as each part retains its motion, and communicates it, as before, to the others.'

be the cause. This is what comes out of Proposition 2 of *Ethics* III, according to which 'the Body cannot determine the Mind to thinking, and the Mind cannot determine the Body to motion, to rest, or to anything else (if there is anything else)'. It must be noted that the last detail, 'or to anything else (if there is anything else)', is put forward only for the mind and has no counterpart for the body. It is possible to interpret it not only as a rhetorical expression intended to radicalise the statement and to eliminate any possibility of reciprocal determination, but also as a hint of a reversal or an implicit critique of his previous arguments in the *Short Treatise*, where Spinoza still contemplated the possibility of the soul to deviate, but not produce, the movement of the animal spirits in another direction. Similarly, in the *Ethics*, the perception of the body by the soul no longer appears as an effect of the body but, rather, it is carried out through the ideas of the body's affections, which are in God insofar as he constitutes the nature of our mind, and consequently they are necessarily found in ourselves.[7]

The definition of the affects in the *Ethics* therefore marks a turning point, since it is no longer a question of accepting that mind and body can act on each other in any way whatsoever. The 'mixed' discourse it promotes is thus not an interactive one. Although it re-examines the power of acting and being acted upon of the mind and body together, as in Descartes, what makes all the difference is the importance of *simul*. In Spinoza it excludes any reciprocal causality and takes the form of an equivalence and a correspondence between the modes of two different attributes.

Besides the partial survival of the Cartesian conception of causality in the *Short Treatise*, Spinoza also shows the influence of the author of the *Passions of the Soul* by reproducing Descartes' order of enumerating the passions. For Descartes, all passions of the soul are confused ideas, caused, strengthened and maintained by the movement of animal spirits, which arise from the composition of the six primitive emotions: wonder, love, hate, desire, joy and sadness.[8] Yet, when Spinoza lists the main passions that arise from

---

[7] Cf. *Ethics* II, 19 Dem.; *CWS* I, 466–7.
[8] Cf. *Passions of the Soul* II, LXIX.

opinion in the *Short Treatise*,[9] he mentions above all wonder (*verwondering*), love, hate and desire.

This listing is very far from that of the *Ethics*, since in that work, desire, which is last in the *Short Treatise*'s list, comes first and takes centre stage, not only by virtue of its status as a primitive affect but also by virtue of its nature, which expresses the very essence of humanity, in that it is determined to produce the things necessary for the preservation of humankind. In addition, joy and sadness, which in the *Ethics* are the only two other primitive affects apart from desire, are not even mentioned as examples of the main affects in Chapter II of *Short Treatise* II, and are only analysed in Chapter V. Wonder, which enjoyed pride of place in the *Short Treatise*, in line with the Cartesian model, is demoted to the rank of simple affection and disappears from the list of affects in the *Ethics*.[10]

The question, then, is to find out when, how and why this transformation in the conception of the affects occurred. To be sure, it is not a question of reducing the *Short Treatise* to a Cartesian text, since Spinoza started distancing himself from the author of the *Principles* in this work. The definition of the proximate and principal cause of the passions is not the body, and the exercise of reciprocal causality remains an exception. It is, however, a question of understanding how Spinoza came to his original conception of the affects.

From this point of view, the *Theological-Political Treatise* appears to be a key analytical tool, since by virtue of the strategic place it occupies in the structure of the system, it may be seen as an intermediary and may provide material that can shed light on the origin of the definitive text. Published in 1670 – although the exact date it was written is not known with certainty – it is situated in the transitional period between the youthful work that is the *Short Treatise* and the complete work that is the *Ethics*, which was published in 1677 after Spinoza's death. From its position between the two, the *Theological-Political Treatise* may offer an interesting perspective on the progression of Spinoza's thought and on the development of his new ideas concerning the affects and the prin-

---

[9] *KV* II, 3; *CWS* I, 99–102.
[10] Cf. *Ethics* III, DA 4, Exp.; *CWS* I, 532.

ciple of their enumeration. It is a milestone likely to attest to both the break with Descartes, which was not yet complete in the *Short Treatise*, and to how Spinoza reworked concepts over time. That is why we need to compare this work with the *Ethics*.

Beyond its role as a tool to assess Spinoza's development, it can also be useful for a second reason. Even though the *Theological-Political Treatise* does not have the express goal of analysing the nature and origin of the affects, its Preface opens with a description of the behaviour of humans fallen prey to the vicissitudes of fortune; it brings to light their various feelings so that it resembles a historical account of the origin of the affects, or at least an attempt to describe how the passions arose in humankind in the real world. From this point of view it offers an interesting perspective in understanding the affects, since it does not espouse the geometric deduction of the affects, which goes from the simple to the complex, from primary affects to their combinations. Instead, it recounts their first appearance and how they were generated according to circumstances and historical events. It is therefore better able to get across the idea of a real human being caught in a web of relationships with the outside world. While the *Ethics* develops a geometric psychophysiology of the affects, the analyses of the *Theological-Political Treatise* are closer to what Kant would call a pragmatic anthropology of the affects. The Preface's method of reasoning demonstrates this, since it combines deductions and arguments with empirical observations,[11] as well as with historical examples such as that of Alexander the Great.[12] Under these circumstances, it may be interesting to compare and contrast these two approaches and to examine the meaning and significance of the differences. We may then determine whether the differences are evidence of a simple change in points of view that are compatible with one another, or whether they reveal divergences indicating a transformation in Spinoza's thought.

[11] Cf. for example, *TTP* Praef. 2; CWS II, 66: '*For no one who has lived among men has failed to see* that when they are prospering, even if they are quite inexperienced, they are generally so full of their own wisdom that they think themselves wronged if anyone wants to give them advice.' Emphasis added.

[12] *TTP* Praef. 5; CWS II, 67.

The Principles of the Comparison

Comparing the origin of the affects in the Preface to the *Theological-Political Treatise* and their *more geometrico* deduction in the *Ethics* may seem pointless at first glance, since the two works have neither the same objective nor the same status, making comparison difficult. While Spinoza explicitly aims to determine the nature and origin of the affects in *Ethics* III, apparently there is no equivalent undertaking in the *Theological-Political Treatise*. Strictly speaking, the latter work does not include a theory of affects. It is simply punctuated with comments on the subject that do not assume a pre-existing general doctrine, as is the case in the *Political Treatise*, where Spinoza summarises the key features of his system, laying out and explaining the basic concepts by briefly demonstrating them again, so that his points are understandable without having to refer to previous texts.[13] Thus, for example, in Chapters I and II of the *Political Treatise*, the author recalls the conception of the passions developed in the *Ethics* and expressly refers to it.[14] There is nothing like it in the *Theological-Political Treatise*, so we must reconstruct the theory of the affects, if indeed there is one, on the basis of isolated comments and occasional observations by Spinoza. The absence of such a theory, however, should not be over-interpreted, since the *Theological-Political Treatise* does not expressly aim to determine the essence of the affects but, rather, to demonstrate the compatibility of individuals' freedom of thought with the theological and political authorities, as well as the need for this freedom to safeguard peace and piety.

Although setting up his argument entails examining the relationship between philosophy and theology, on the one hand, and between philosophy and politics, on the other, it does not call for a systematic study of the affects but, rather, simply a limited analysis of certain passions that either harm or benefit freedom of thought and civil order. Spinoza therefore only uses what is necessary for the structure of his message, and consequently, it is not at all surprising that he does not devote a chapter or a part of his

[13] Cf. *TP* II, 1; *CWS* II, 507.
[14] *TP* I, 5; *CWS* II, 505–6 and II, 1; *CWS* II, 507.

work to analysing the affects, as he had done in the *Short Treatise*, or as he would do in the *Ethics*.

Though comparing the two works is risky, given that the *Ethics* and the *Theological-Political Treatise* are not situated in the same speculative space, it is nevertheless possible, as long as we systematically cross-check the conclusions of such a comparison against the difference in genres, to verify whether the divergences are solely explained by the requirements of their respective arguments and the nature of the subject, or whether they are evidence of evolution in Spinoza's thought. Since the *Theological-Political Treatise* does not have a theory on the subject, it will involve determining the main characteristics of the affects as they are stated in the *Ethics*, and using them as a standard against which we can measure the disparities between the two works. We can thus analyse the progression of Spinoza's thought on the basis of three key points of comparison: the definition of the affects; their causes; and the principle of their enumeration.

The Principles of the Definition and Enumeration of the Affects in the *Ethics*

The theory of affects put forward in Part III of the *Ethics* is presented, as we know, according to the geometric order prevailing in the work as a whole. In line with the requirements of the Euclidean model of proof, Spinoza begins by formulating the definition of affect, then groups it together with both the affections of the body that have repercussions on the power of acting and the ideas of these affections.

Now, according to Spinoza's *On the Emendation of the Intellect*, the proper definition of a created thing or of a mode, to take up the vocabulary used in the *Ethics*, must fulfil three main criteria. First, it must express the inmost essence of the thing.[15] Second, it must include its proximate cause.[16] The proximate cause is the cause that immediately produces the thing. It is not a question of getting into an infinite regress and examining the cause of the proximate

---

[15] *TdIE* 95; *CWS* I, 39.
[16] *TdIE* 96; *CWS* I, 39–40.

cause, and so on ad infinitum. If all finite modes are the result of an infinite series of finite causes, it is enough just to mention the proximate cause in order to explain its essence, it being understood that God and his attributes are the cause of all things. That is why the proper definition of a circle does not cover the series of causes that can produce its existence but stops at the idea of a segment, one of whose extremities is fixed and the other mobile – an idea that is sufficient to highlight how it is generated. Third, the definition of the thing must be such that 'all its properties can be inferred from its definition'.[17]

Definition 3 of Part III confirms these requirements, since it is not limited to expressing the essence of the affects but also determines their proximate cause. Indeed, Spinoza points out that the affect is the result of either an adequate cause, in which case it is an action, or of an inadequate cause, in which case it is a passion. This definition, at any rate, is of such a nature that all properties of affects can be deduced from it. It is enough to analyse it to see that it implicitly contains all the characteristics of the affects that will be deduced in Parts III, IV and V of the *Ethics*. Thus, by dealing with the concept of adequate cause in depth and by bringing to light its ultimate implications, it is possible to understand the cause of the passions, attributing it to the fact that humankind is only a part of nature and likely to undergo changes other than those that can be explained solely by its essence. The inadequate cause, since it is a partial cause whose effect cannot be understood only through itself,[18] involves the cooperation of other external causes, and consequently invites us to conceptualise the agent as a mode determined by other modes within *Natura naturata*.

In addition, by analysing the definition of affect itself, it is possible to deduce the existence of the three primitive affects. Although they are not explicitly mentioned, desire, joy, and sadness are contained in Definition 3. Indeed, joy and sadness are respectively presented in the form of an increase or decrease in the power of acting. Desire can be deduced from the power of

---

[17] *TdIE* 97; *CWS* I, 40. Translation modified.
[18] Cf. *Ethics* III, Def. 1; *CWS* I, 492.

acting itself, as it takes the form of striving to persevere in being and opposing anything contrary to it. Now, this striving, when it is related to the mind and body together, is called appetite, and desire, when it is accompanied by consciousness of it.[19] The concept of the power of acting, as it appears in Definition 3, therefore covers desire.

Once desire, joy and sadness are deduced from the existence of a power of acting that is capable of withstanding quite a few changes, making it pass sometimes to greater, sometimes to a lesser perfection, Spinoza can construct the entire geometry of affects by using the linear model made up of the primary trio of affects and enter into the second dimension. More complex affects, which put into play inconstant relationships with an external cause, are added on top of the primary affects that only relate to the perfection of mankind. Thus love and hate, hope and fear, confidence and despair, gladness and remorse come into being.[20] At a later stage of composition and growing complexity, affects such as pity, favour, indignation and envy appear, which are created from the affects of others when the external cause takes the form of a fellow human being and induces affective imitation.

Without going into a complete listing of the affects, then, it is possible to compare the *Theological-Political Treatise* and the *Ethics* on three points: the definition of the affects, the nature of their cause that makes it possible to distinguish actions from passions, and the principle of their enumeration.

The Principles of the Concept of Affect in the *Theological-Political Treatise*

This task, however, comes up against three obstacles. First, in the *Theological-Political Treatise* the concept of affect is not properly defined. Second, its various types are not expressly differentiated by virtue of the nature of the knowledge they involve, as is also the case in the *Short Treatise* and in the *Ethics*. Third, there is no enumeration of the 'principal' affects in the *Short Treatise*, or of

[19] Cf. *Ethics* III, 9 Schol.; CWS I, 500.
[20] Cf. *Ethics* III, 18 Schol. 2; CWS I, 505.

the 'primary' or 'primitive' affects in the *Ethics*. Does this mean that any attempt at comparison is doomed to failure?

The absence of a definition, subdivision or enumeration is not necessarily an impediment. At best it calls for prudence, but it is not an insurmountable obstacle since, on the one hand, it is possible in theory to reconstruct a definition on the basis of sparse information and, on the other, the Preface to the *Treatise* offers an account of how the affects originated in practice. That is why, logically, we must reverse the order of analysis and start by examining the principles governing how we inventory the affects, since this is the focus of Spinoza's reflection and he provides us with the most material on this subject.

The Origin of the Affects in the Preface

In the Preface to the *Theological-Political Treatise*, Spinoza analyses the behaviour of people faced with the vagaries of fortune or unfavourable circumstances. He gives the reasons why they generally fall prey to superstition, deducing them from a set of affects that do not exactly cover the primitive trio of desire, joy and sadness of the *Ethics*.

Admittedly, as early as paragraph 1, it is clear that *cupiditas* appears to be fundamental. All the complex affects are rooted first and foremost in the desire for things. But here it is about an excessive desire for uncertain things. People 'immoderately desire (*cupiant sino modo*)', Spinoza tells us, reiterating this assertion in paragraph 4. The term *cupiditas*, as such, appears infrequently in the *Theological-Political Treatise*. It is often replaced with the term *libido*, or concupiscence.

The combination of this unbridled desire with the vicissitudes of fortune necessarily produces a pair of fluctuating affects, depending on whether fate has been favourable or unfavourable. Thus, immoderate desire is accompanied by either hope or fear, depending on whether fortune tilts one way or another. When fears are quelled and hope becomes certainty, it is accompanied by pride or overconfidence (*praefidens*) and pomposity.

This triumvirate of immoderate desire, fear and pride, which does not match the trio of primitive affects in the *Ethics*, is reminiscent of the three basic passions that Thomas Hobbes attributed to humankind in the state of nature, and which would bring about war of all against all. In Chapter VI of Book I of his work *De Cive* (1642), Hobbes paints a portrait of humankind inclined to fear, glory and the desire for things.

To be sure, in Hobbes fear is the dominant passion, while in Spinoza it is immoderate desire. However, the difference is less marked than would appear, for two reasons. On the one hand, Hobbes recognises that the desire to look for things for the purposes of self-preservation is primary and is the foundation of the law of nature:

> Every man is desirous of what is good for him, and shuns what is evil, but chiefly the chiefest of natural evils, which is Death; and this he doth, by a certain impulsion of nature, no less than that whereby a Stone moves downward [. . .] Therefore the first foundation of natural Right is this, That every man as much as in him lies endeavour to protect his life and members.[21]

The mutual fear at the root of civil society is a consequence of the desire for self-preservation. It arises in part from the observation that all people are equal and are equally capable of killing one another by force or cunning, and in part from the existence of a desire to harm due to the arrogance of some people who believe themselves superior to others.[22] On the other hand, in the Preface to the *Theological-Political Treatise*, Spinoza assigns a leading role to fear, making it 'the most powerful of the affects'.[23] It is what causes, maintains and feeds superstition, so that it is the source of many conflicts.

Consequently, although the *Theological-Political Treatise* breaks with the categorisation of the passions in the *Short Treatise*, which remains partially Cartesian, it corresponds to what we might call a Hobbesian phase in Spinoza's thought, but one that no longer appears as such in the *Ethics*.

---

[21] *De Cive*, Section I, Ch. I, VII.
[22] *De Cive*, Section I, Ch. I, III, and IV.
[23] *TTP* Praef. 7; CWS II, 68. Translation modified.

Fear, an affect derived from sadness in the *Ethics* and set in fourth position after love, hate and hope, appears as a primitive affect in the *Theological-Political Treatise*, since it is from fear that all the other affects listed by Spinoza in the Preface are derived. Fear as a generator of superstitions will be accompanied by inconstant affects, depending on whether circumstances are more or less favourable. Indeed, superstition cannot maintain itself without hope, hate, anger and cunning. Fear can thus become more extreme and transform into dread or become coloured with hope, feeding hatred and anger against scapegoats. It leads people to look for signs or omens to reassure themselves and ward off bad luck. It makes them astonished by things that are out of the ordinary, which are then interpreted as phenomena indicating the anger of the gods. Wonder appears in the Preface as a leading affect. Coupled with fear, wonder plays a dominant role in reinforcing superstition and leads to the folly of interpreting nature.[24] The key status given to wonder in the Preface has no equivalent in the *Ethics*, where its role is minor: not only does it not appear among the primitive affects, as in the *Short Treatise*, but Spinoza no longer even considers it to be an affect.

Exploited politically to govern the multitude, superstitious fear can in turn give rise to two opposite passions, devotion and hatred, depending on the rulers' interests. Quoting Quintus Curtius Rufus, Spinoza remarks:

Nothing governs the multitude more effectively than superstition. That's why they are easily led, under the pretext of religion, now to worship their kings as gods, now to curse and loathe them as the common plague of the human race.[25]

Generally speaking, the origin of the affects described in the Preface leaves little room for positive feelings and brings to light what the *Ethics* will later present as sad passions. Spinoza highlights the predominance of hate, ambition, envy and sordid greed. He relegates love, joy and good faith to the rank of Christian

[24] *TTP* Praef. 3; *CWS* II, 66.
[25] *TTP* Praef. 8; *CWS* II, 68.

ideals that are hardly ever put into practice, because the people who boast about professing them are more likely to 'contend so unfairly against one another, and indulge daily in the bitterest hatred toward one another, so that each man's faith is known more easily from his hatred and contentiousness than from his love, gladness, etc.'.[26]

When all is said and done, the first affects emerging in the Preface – unbridled desire, fear and pride – are different from the primary affects in the *Ethics* on the one hand and, on the other, the derived affects – wonder, devotion, and hate – are to be relegated to the background for at least two of them. Although hate is omnipresent, love, by contrast, is conspicuously absent.

The question is whether these disparities are due to differences in objectives and the method of presentation, or whether they reflect a profound divergence and an evolution in Spinoza's thought on the subject. The origin of the affects in the Preface is without doubt more in line with historical reality and based on the observations of experience. It is hardly surprising, indeed, to see fear, immoderate desire and pride reigning supreme over ignorant minds tossed about by the winds of fate. The *Ethics*, incidentally, does not disavow these fully realistic analyses. However, by proceeding geometrically, it most often discovers the affects by pairs of opposites and puts them on an equal footing, although they do not occur with the same frequency in reality. *More geometrico* deduction conceives of affects rarely found in reality. This is the case with cheerfulness, for example, which is more easily conceived than observed, since it implies that all parts of the body are equally affected by joy.

Although, at first glance, there is no reason to pit the two concepts against each other or to consider them to be incompatible despite their differences, it must be noted that the *Theological-Political Treatise* lingers over the passions and does not mention the active affects as the *Ethics* does. It is therefore a question of whether, beyond the realism that philosophy must demonstrate on the subject of politics, Spinoza considers all the affects to be passions and whether he does not accept the existence of actions,

[26] *TTP* Praef. 14; *CWS* II, 70.

in the technical sense of the term. With this in mind, it is important to determine the nature of affect in the *Theological-Political Treatise*.

Defining 'Affect' in the Theological-Political Treatise

Although the concept of affect is not expressly defined in the work, it is possible to reconstruct its meaning on the basis of its occurrences. The term appears for the first time in the Preface in paragraph 7, when Spinoza maintains that superstition 'arises, not from reason, but only from the most powerful affects (*non ex ratione sed solo affectu eoque efficacissimo*)'.[27] The word 'affect' here takes on the meaning of passion and appears to be contrasted to reason. Logically, Spinoza should have used the word '*passio*'; yet here he uses '*affectus*' as if all affects were passional and could not have a rational origin.

This appearance of the term 'affect' to refer to passion, or any impulse not arising from reason, is not an isolated occurrence. Spinoza systematically uses this word every time he deals with a feeling that is contrary to reason. This is what happens, for example, in paragraph 34 of the Preface, when the author brings up the common people 'or anyone else who is struggling with the same affects as the common people (*vulgus ergo et omnes, qui cum vulgo iisdem affectibus conflictantur*)'.[28] This use of the word affect as a synonym for passion does not only occur in the Preface, where it is hardly surprising that the two terms overlap, seeing that it examines the superstitious attitudes of people buffeted by fate. It is also used in Chapter V, where Spinoza proclaims:

> Everyone seeks his own advantage – but people want things and judge them useful, not by the dictate of sound reason, but for the most part only from immoderate desire and because they are carried away by affects of mind (*et animi affectibus abrepti*), which take no account of the future and of other things.[29]

---

[27] *TTP* Praef. 7; *CWS* II, 68.
[28] *TTP* Praef. 34; *CWS* II, 75.
[29] *TTP* V, 21; *CWS* II, 144.

In addition, it is found in Chapter XV[30] on two occasions, then in Chapter XVI, where Spinoza mentions 'whatever anyone who is considered to be only under the rule of nature judges to be useful for himself – whether under the guidance of sound reason or by the prompting of the affects (*affectus impetu*)',[31] and finally in Chapter XVII, where the appearance of the word *affectus* either concludes a list of passions[32] or serves as a counterweight to the command of reason.[33]

The presence of the word 'affect' cannot be explained by the term 'passion' not being part of Spinoza's vocabulary in the *Theological-Political Treatise*. Indeed, in paragraph 7 of Chapter XVII the noun '*passio*' is used several lines after the first occurrence of the word '*affectus*' and a few lines before the second, when the author defines respect as 'a passion (*passio*) composed of fear and wonder'.[34]

Although it is by no means exhaustive, the list of occurrences of the word '*affectus*' makes it possible to map out the scope of the concept and to limit it to passive feelings and impulses of which the individual is a partial cause. In the absence of any indication to the contrary, there is every reason to believe that in the *Theological-Political Treatise* passion and affect are synonymous

---

[30] *TTP* XV, 40; *CWS* II, 281: 'For we can easily show that they say this either from the affects or from vain-glory (*vel ex affectibus vel vana gloria*).' *TTP* XV, 42; *CWS* II, 281: 'He's speaking only from a prejudice stemming from his affects (*affectuum praejudicio*).'

[31] *TTP* XVI, 8; *CWS* II, 284.

[32] *TTP* XVII, 6; *CWS* II, 297: 'For whatever reason a man resolves to carry out the commands of the supreme power, whether because he fears punishment, or because he hopes for something from it, or because he loves his Country, or because he has been impelled by any other affect whatever (*sive alio quocunque affectu impulsus*).' *TTP* XVII, 10; *CWS* II, 298: 'So without any intellectual incoherence, we can conceive men who believe, love, hate, disdain, or are overcome by any kind of affect whatever (*absolute nullo non affectu*), solely in accordance with the right of the state.'

[33] *TTP* XVII, 14; *CWS* II, 298–9: 'Those who've experienced how changeable the mentality of the multitude is almost despair about it. They're governed only by affects, not by reason (*quia non ratione, sed solis affectibus gubernatur*).'

[34] *TTP* XVII, 7; *CWS* II, 297.

and interchangeable, and that the first is not simply a form of the second but, rather, that they overlap entirely.

Does this then mean that the crucial distinction between actions and passions that Spinoza introduces in Definition 3 of *Ethics* III is completely absent from the *Theological-Political Treatise*, and that the affects, including when they result from true knowledge, are always characterised by passivity? Is the existence of active affects an innovation of the *Ethics*, or can it already be found in the *Theological-Political Treatise*, even though Spinoza is silent on the subject there, given that he deals above all with the affects of the common people, whose passionate nature is beyond doubt? The issue is a major one, since in the *Short Treatise* the affects as a whole are marked by passivity, including when they fall under distinct knowledge. Indeed, whether the affects originate from opinion, belief or clear knowledge, the fact remains that they are passions. This stems from the idea that the intellect is wholly passive, so that truth is not a product of the mind but a modification of thought resulting from an action carried out by the whole object.[35] Thus, love is presented as a passion that arises from report and opinion just as much as from true ideas.[36] Should we then consider that this classic conception of knowledge and the affects is still valid in the *Theological-Political Treatise*?

Do Actions Exist in the Theological-Political Treatise?

To avoid drawing hasty conclusions, we must examine the way in which the *Theological-Political Treatise* presents the feelings called 'active affects' in the *Ethics*. In Proposition 59 of Part III, active affects related to the mind, insofar as it understands, are grouped together under the category of *fortitudo*, or strength of character, which is subdivided into firmness (*animositas*) and generosity (*generositas*). Firmness is the action that aims to preserve the agent's

---

[35] Cf. *KV* II, 15, 5; *CWS* I, 120: 'To grasp this better, note that the intellect (though the word sounds otherwise) is wholly *passive*, that is, that our soul is changed in such a way that it acquires other modes of thinking it did not have before.'
[36] Cf. *KV* II, 3, 4; *CWS* I, 100.

being and advantage. It encompasses moderation, sobriety and presence of mind, among others. Generosity has to do with the preservation and advantage of other people; it includes courtesy and mercy.

Yet we must note that the concepts of *fortitudo*, *animositas* and *generositas* hardly appear in the *Theological-Political Treatise*. Among the virtuous inclinations, justice and charity take centre stage and are presented as the results of people living either under the command of religion or guided by reason. Yet neither charity nor justice is presented as an affect. Although the concept of justice appears in *Ethics* IV, such as in Scholium 2 of Proposition 37, charity (*caritas*) is missing. Admittedly, charity, as it implies abiding by the golden rule to love thy neighbour, is rooted in religion above all, but this is not enough to explain its absence in the *Ethics*. Morality and compassion are mentioned,[37] by way of a redefinition. Why does the same not apply to charity, which could be included among the good passions since it is not part of the active affects? We should therefore examine this aspect of the *Theological-Political Treatise*, which makes justice and charity the crux of salvation, so much so that the figure of the righteous individual appears to take precedence over the figure of the wise man. Thus, while *Ethics* V closes with the distinction between the wise man and the ignorant one, the last chapter of the *Theological-Political Treatise*[38] contrasts honest and free-minded people with evildoers and scoundrels.

Although the case of active affects categorised in the *Ethics* as *fortitudo* is not very convincing, inasmuch as it does not have an equivalent in the *Theological-Political Treatise*, the case of the love of God, on the other hand, is likely to be more illuminating,

---

[37] In *Ethics* III, DA 24, compassion is grouped together with 'Love, insofar as it so affects a man that he is glad at another's good fortune, and saddened by his ill fortune'; morality (*pietas*) is presented in *Ethics* IV, 37 Schol. 1; CWS I, 565–6, as 'the Desire to do good generated in us by our living according to the guidance of reason'.

[38] TTP XX, 30; CWS II, 349: 'laws made concerning opinions aren't concerned with the wicked, but with people who act like free men, that they aren't made to restrain the malicious but to aggravate honest men (*honestos*)'.

since it appears in both works. Indeed, in paragraphs 9 to 19 of Chapter IV of the *Treatise* Spinoza alludes to the love of God,[39] which in the *Ethics* can be alternately a passion, when it takes the form of an imaginary superstitious representation or devotion bordering on idolatry, or, on the contrary, an action called either *amor erga Deum*[40] or *amor intellectualis Deum*,[41] depending on whether it results from the second or third kind of knowledge. In the *Theological-Political Treatise*, Spinoza also distinguishes the love of God arising from the imagination from one stemming from true knowledge, which is the supreme good. Nonetheless, although he accepts that 'the knowledge and love of God is the ultimate end towards which all our actions ought to be directed',[42] he never expressly presents *amor Dei* as an active affect. It must be noted, for that matter, that the concept of the love of God is by no means subdivided into two categories depending on whether it arises from reason or intuitive knowledge. Neither do the expressions '*amor erga Deum*' and '*amor intellectualis Deum*' appear. Only *amor Dei* appears without there ever being question of a distinction between passion and action on the one hand and the various rational and intuitive forms of the action on the other. In Chapter IV the supreme good and happiness are always defined by the knowledge and love of God,[43] without the two components being condensed under the expression 'the intellectual love of God'.

Against this background it is possible to question whether Spinoza's silence on the subject stems from a deliberate omission, or whether the distinction between active and passive affects is an innovation specific to the *Ethics*. It must be recognised that, in his formulation, Spinoza's conception in the *Theological-Political*

---

[39] Cf. *TTP* IV, 9; *CWS* II, 127, *TTP* IV, 12; *CWS* II, 128, *TTP* IV, 14; *CWS* II, 128, *TTP* IV, 15; *CWS* II, 129, *TTP* IV, 19; *CWS* II, 129–30.

[40] *Ethics* V, 15; *CWS* I, 603.

[41] *Ethics* V, 32 Cor.; *CWS* I, 611.

[42] *TTP* IV, 15; *CWS* I, 129.

[43] Cf. *TTP* IV, 9; *CWS* II, 127: 'the supreme good, that is, *the true knowledge and love of God*'; *TTP* IV, 11; *CWS* II, 128: 'Our supreme good, then, and our blessedness come back to this: the *knowledge and love of God*'; *TTP* IV, 15; *CWS* II, 129: 'The *knowledge and love of God* is the ultimate end.' Emphasis added.

Treatise remains very close to the *Short Treatise*'s, where the affects are all considered to be passions regardless of their cognitive origin. Indeed, in the latter work, happiness and blessedness also consist in the knowledge and love of God[44] without reference to the concept of the intellectual love of God. The examination of this one particular case of the love of God, however, does not allow us to draw general conclusions. That is why it is necessary to check whether the same phenomenon recurs for other types of affects.

Paragraph 50 of Chapter V of the *Theological-Political Treatise* can serve as a decisive test in this regard. Here, Spinoza concludes his point by listing some of the mind's inclinations for achieving happiness, which may be similar to the active affects in the *Ethics*:

> We cannot know anyone except by his works (*operibus*). Therefore, if a man is rich in these fruits, loving kindness, gladness (*gaudium*), peace, patience, beneficence, goodness, good faith, gentleness and self-restraint – against which (as Paul says in Galatians 5:22) there is no law – whether he has been taught only by reason or only by Scripture, he has truly been taught by God and is completely blessed.

This text is of considerable interest for our argument for two reasons. On the one hand it lists the inclinations and the affects that cover the distinction made in the *Ethics* between actions and passions, because they stem from reason as well as from Scripture – that is, from an authority that, for Spinoza, calls on imaginative knowledge. On the other hand, some of the affects mentioned, such as *gaudium* and good faith (*fide*) are found in the *Ethics*,[45] and are considered to be active affects when they arise from reason and the mind is their adequate cause.

We must then note that in paragraph 50 the affects likely to be

---

[44] Cf. *KV* II, 26, 2; *CWS* I, 146: 'Before we can attain to the knowledge, and consequently, to the *love, of God*'; *KV* II, 26, 3; *CWS* I, 146: 'The power of *knowledge and divine love*'; *KV* II, 26, 5; *CWS* I, 146–7: 'Unless we have first arrived at *the knowledge and love of God*'. Emphasis added.

[45] *Gaudium*: cf. *Ethics* III, DA 16; *CWS* I, 535; *Ethics* V, 42; *CWS* I, 616; *fide*: *Ethics* IV, 72; *CWS* I, 586: 'A free man always acts in good faith (*cum fide*).' Translation modified.

passions or actions, depending on whether the person has been taught by Scripture alone or reason alone, are not presented as such. They are grouped together with works or fruits. Spinoza thus does not return to the distinction between action and passion, according to whether the inclinations are peculiar to the person taught by reason alone or Scripture alone; instead, he subsumes them under the single category of work. The concept of work therefore transcends the distinction between action and passion, and cannot be understood as the strict equivalent of a product of an adequate cause, since it also covers the fruits of abiding by the golden rule to love thy neighbour, as dictated by Scripture.

In reality, as Spinoza indicates, this concept is borrowed from the Apostle Paul, who shows in his *Epistle to the Galatians* that works are the fruit of the Holy Spirit. Moreover, Spinoza refers to the Apostle at greater length in Chapter XV:

> For from Chapter 14 it follows as clearly as can be that the Holy Spirit gives testimony only concerning good works (*bonis operibus*). That's why even Paul calls them the fruit of the Holy Spirit (Galatians 5:22). Really, the Holy Spirit is nothing but a satisfaction that arises in the mind from good actions (*bonis actionibus*).[46]

This passage is interesting in more ways than one. First, it confirms the fact that the term 'works' has a broader meaning than 'actions', since Spinoza, while being careful to point out that the Holy Spirit gives testimony only about good works, implies that there are bad ones as well. Consequently, the concept of work covers the fruits of reason as well as the fruits of joyous or sad passions. Second, he establishes a connection between the concepts of work, to which the affects listed in paragraph 50 of Chapter V are reducible, and of good action. It can therefore give credence to the idea that in the *Theological-Political Treatise* Spinoza was already making a distinction between actions and passions. The real question is whether the term 'actions' takes on the same meaning here as in Definition 3 of *Ethics* III.

[46] *TTP* XV, 41; CWS II, 281.

There is nothing to confirm it; some indications even suggest the opposite. Indeed, once again, mentioning 'good' actions
implies that some are not. Yet the affects that are actions in the
Ethics cannot be bad. Arising from reason, they are always useful
and express the agreement of humans in nature.[47] Moreover, the
relationship between these good actions and the fruits of the Holy
Spirit prevents us from understanding them solely as products of
adequate causes, since they can also fall under the guidance of
reason or obedience to Scripture.

On the basis of an examination of these affects presented as
works linked to the exercise of reason as well as faith, it is therefore impossible to decide in favour of the existence of actions in
the technical sense of the term. Does this mean that we should
consider that Spinoza did not yet have this conceptual device and
that he developed it at a later date?

Although it is difficult to resolve this question inasmuch as
it comes down to interpreting a silence, it is no longer possible
in the present case to invoke the fact that the two works do not
have the same aim. We also cannot make the argument that it is
unnecessary in the *Theological-Political Treatise* to analyse in detail
the different types of affects since, in paragraph 50 of Chapter V,
Spinoza fittingly makes a distinction between works falling under
the teachings of reason and those falling under the teachings of
Scripture, which matches the distinction the *Ethics* establishes
between actions and passions. It is thus quite surprising that
Spinoza himself does not mention this simple distinction here,
given that it is called for, literally speaking.

We must note in this respect that the *Political Treatise*, which
also does not aim to develop a science of the affects, restricting
itself to a review of knowledge useful in understanding the origin
and nature of the state, uses this distinction between action and
passion. Spinoza is thus careful to draw our attention to the fact
that 'desires which don't arise from reason are not so much human
actions as passions'.[48]

There is therefore every reason to believe that Spinoza had not

---

[47] Cf. *Ethics* IV, 35; CWS I, 563.
[48] *TP* II, 5; CWS II, 508–9.

yet developed the distinction between active and passive affects in the *Political-Theological Treatise,* and that the *Ethics* ushers in a new concept of the affects and their relationship to reason.

Reason and Appetite in the *Theological-Political Treatise*

The hypothesis discussed above is supported by the fact that in the *Theological-Political Treatise* appetite and desire are systematically contrasted with reason. They only cover passionate striving and obey laws that mostly enter into conflict with the laws of reason. This is what emerges from Chapter XVI, where the impulses of appetite are juxtaposed against the laws of reason alone:

> So among men who are considered as living only under the rule of nature, one who does not yet know reason, or does not yet have a habit of virtue, has a supreme right to live according to the laws of appetite alone – just as much as one who guides his life according to the laws of reason.[49]

This contrast between the laws of appetite and reason occurs throughout Chapter XVI,[50] and it reappears in Chapter XIX:

> For we've shown in Chapter XVI that in the state of nature reason has no more right than appetite, but that both those who live according to the laws of appetite and those who live

[49] *TTP* XVI, 6; *CWS* II, 283.
[50] Cf. *TTP* XVI, 14; *CWS* II, 285: 'To live, not only securely, but very well, men had to agree in having one purpose. So they brought it about that they would have collectively the natural right each one had to all things. It would no longer be determined according to the force and appetite of each one, but according to the power and will of everyone together. Nevertheless, they would have tried this in vain if they wanted to follow only what appetite urges. For according to the laws of appetite each person is drawn in a different direction. So they had to make a very firm resolution and contract to direct everything only according to the dictate of reason.' Cf. *TTP* XVI, 52; *CWS* II, 292: 'Anyone in the state of nature who doesn't have the use of reason lives, by the supreme right of nature, according to the laws of appetite.'

according to the laws of reason have the right to do whatever they can.[51]

It is reiterated with a contrast between reason and desire in paragraph 7 of Chapter XVI: 'The natural right of each man is determined not by sound reason, but by desire and power (*non sana ratione, sed cupiditate et potentia determinatur*).'[52]

This contrast is so radical that it seems to take the form of an antagonism between two naturally incompatible ways of life. This is highlighted in a curious passage from Chapter XVI:

> For not all men are naturally determined to operate according to the rules and laws of reason. On the contrary, everyone is born ignorant of everything. Before men can know the true principle of living and acquire a virtuous disposition, much of their life has passed, even if they have been well brought up. Meanwhile, they are bound to live, and to preserve themselves, as far as they can by their own power, that is, by the prompting of appetite alone. Nature has given them nothing else. It has denied them the actual power to live according to sound reason. So they're no more bound to live according to the laws of a sound mind than a cat is bound to live according to the laws of a lion's nature.[53]

It would appear that humankind is constituted of two parts, appetite and reason, which are difficult to reconcile. It is subject to two systems of natural laws: the natural laws of appetite and the natural laws of reason, which alternate, one or the other prevailing in turn, in proportion to one's ignorance or education. This duality of laws introduces a duality of nature and raises the problem of going from a way of life based on passion to a rational

---

[51] *TTP* XIX, 7; CWS II, 333–4.

[52] *TTP* XVI, 7; CWS II, 283. It must be noted here that not only *cupiditas* but also *potentia* are contrasted with reason. This proves that the systematic distinction between *potestas*, understood as bad power, an arbitrary and despotic power related to passion, and *potentia*, or true power, is not relevant, because here *potentia* is contrasted with reason.

[53] *TTP* XVI, 7; CWS II, 283.

one. Changing the system would appear to be impossible, as the analogy of the metamorphosis of the cat into a lion would suggest. Whoever lives by the laws of appetite is no more obliged to live by the laws of a sound mind than a cat is by the laws of a lion's nature, Spinoza tells us. Is not changing one's way of life and going from appetite to reason tantamount to changing one's nature, and a cat becoming a lion? An impossible task if ever there was one.

Does this mean that there are two natures, one based on appetite and the other rational, and that the essence of humanity is marked by this duality? Spinoza does not go that far, but his comparison is rather curious all the same, since it suggests that the difference between the fool and the rational person is less a difference of degree than of nature, and that an almost unbridgeable gap separates them. Moreover, in an analogous passage in the *Political Treatise*, Spinoza does not go back to this problematic comparison between the fool and the wise man and the cat and the lion, but opts for one of illness and good health, which does not imply a difference of nature: 'So the ignorant and weak-minded are no more bound by the Law of nature to organise their lives wisely than a sick man is bound to have a sound Body.'[54]

The fact remains that, in the *Theological Political Treatise*, reason and the affects remain in a relationship of exteriority to one another, as if a rational appetite or an 'appetitive' reason could not exist. Neither appetite nor desire are rational in this work, so it is not at all surprising that the affects cannot be conceived as active, and that the distinction between action and passion does not appear.

The *Ethics* breaks with this dual conception of human nature and removes all traces of a divide, by promoting an appetitive reason and a rational appetite. The concept of appetite, as it is defined in Part III, does not take on the same meaning or scope as in the *Theological-Political Treatise*. Whether or not it takes the form of conscious desire, it expresses the very essence of humankind and is nothing other than the effort to persevere in its being as it is related to the mind and body.[55] In the *Ethics*, appetite can

[54] *TP* II, 18; *CWS* II, 515.
[55] Cf. *Ethics* III, 9 Schol.; *CWS* I, 500.

be based on reason or on the passions, depending on whether it is caused by an adequate or inadequate cause. It therefore encompasses any and all striving, regardless of its nature.

The *Ethics* thus offers a more unified vision of humankind, which is only endowed with a single appetitive nature that is at times expressed passively and at other times actively. Spinoza emphasises this point in the Scholium to Proposition 4 of *Ethics* V:

> For it must particularly be noted that the appetite by which a man is said to act, and that by which he is said to be acted on, are one and the same. For example, we have shown that human nature is so constituted that each of us wants the others to live according to his temperament (see III 31S). And indeed, in a man who is not led by reason, this appetite is the passion called Ambition, which does not differ much from Pride. On the other hand, in a man who lives according to the dictate of reason, it is the action or virtue called Morality.

Consequently, in the *Ethics* Spinoza turns anthropological evidence on its head, since he stops pitting reason against appetite in a hostile confrontation. By subsuming actions and passions, as well as all the rules and laws of human nature, under the single concept of appetite, he puts an end to the underlying dualism of the *Political-Theological Treatise*.

Not only does the *Ethics* transform the relationship between reason and appetite by making the first a form of the second, but it also develops a conception of the affects and knowledge that is more dynamic than before. Reason becomes an active power capable of generating affects that constrain the sad passions. While in the *Short Treatise* the intellect is wholly passive, in the *Ethics* it becomes wholly active. Knowledge therefore changes its status, since Spinoza stops thinking of the intellect and its ideas as passive. This transition begins in the *Theological-Political Treatise*, but it is incomplete. Indeed, the power of reason is not as active as in the *Ethics*, because reason appears above all as an authority pronouncing laws that clash with human appetites. Admittedly, in that work, Spinoza assigns to reason the power to form ideas and therefore implicitly recognises its active aspect. This argument, however, is already present in the proponents of a passive intellect, such as in Descartes, where the mind must form innate ideas.

In the *Ethics* Spinoza clearly breaks with Scholastic thought in order to conceptualise ideas as active and dynamic. The definition of an idea as a 'concept of the Mind which the Mind forms because it is a thinking thing'[56] bears traces of it, since Spinoza is careful to point out in the explanation: 'I say concept rather than perception, because the word perception seems to indicate that the Mind is acted on by the object. But concept seems to express an action of the Mind.'

Reason is therefore not characterised by this receptivity that was in the past a guarantee of truth, but by its capacity to produce effects and affects, to form the common notions and the adequate ideas that are the sources of active joy. From this perspective the *Theological-Political Treatise* plays a pivotal role, since it no longer presents knowledge as wholly passive, as in the *Short Treatise*, but neither does it define it as an action. Without being reduced to mute pictures, ideas are still characterised by a certain inertia, while in the *Ethics* they encompass a force of affirmation all the greater since they are adequate.

This difference doubtless stems from the concept of the *conatus*, which is not exactly the same in the two works. In the *Theological-Political Treatise*, 'the supreme law of nature is that each thing strives to persevere in its state (*suo statu*)'.[57] Similarly, the civil right of the citizen is likened to 'the freedom each person has to preserve himself in his state (*in suo statu conservandum*)'.[58] The supreme law of nature in reality corresponds to Descartes' first law of nature, formulated in Part II of *Principles of Philosophy* as 'each and every thing, insofar as it can, always continues in the same state'[59] and is summed up by the principle of inertia and the conservation of momentum. Spinoza's formulation of the *conatus*

---

[56] Cf. *Ethics* II, Def. 3; CWS I, 447.

[57] *TTP* XVI, 3; CWS II, 282–3.

[58] *TTP* XVI, 40; CWS II, 290.

[59] *PP* II, 37. The Latin text is even closer to Spinoza's formulation: '*Prima lex naturae: quod unaquaeque res, quantum in se est, semper in suo statu perseveret; sicque quod semel movetur, semper moveri pergat*' (AT VIII, 72).

in the *Theological-Political Treatise* is therefore a reiteration of a Cartesian statement,[60] which was proved again in Proposition 14 of Part II of *Descartes' Principles of Philosophy*: 'Each thing, insofar as it is simple, undivided, and considered in itself alone, always perseveres in the same state as far as it can.'[61]

In the *Ethics*, on the other hand, the *conatus* is not presented as simple striving to continue in its state, but as striving to persevere in its being (*in suo esse*).[62] The striving to persevere in one's being involves something more than the preservation of the same state, since it is not limited to a simple resistance or to a reproduction of existing effects, but rather consists in expressing all the power of the thing and affirming as much as possible all the properties contained in its essence.

By accentuating the dynamic aspect of the power of acting, by promoting an active and affective reason, the *Ethics* fully expands the theory of the affects and no longer limits it to the sphere of the passions. Part III thus opens a special field of investigation, since it allows us to take the full measure of the nature of humankind and of the psychophysical union, through the indefinite interplay of its actions and passions.

More generally, the evolution of Spinoza's thought after the *Ethics* confirms this orientation of the system towards a more and more dynamic conception of the power of acting. Admittedly, this impression is largely due to a different angle of analysis. The perspective adopted in the *Political Treatise* allows us to better observe the power of acting that is operating in real conditions, where emotions are interconnected and produce complex effects. The theory developed in Part III of the *Ethics*, on the other hand, seeks to identify the fundamental principles that come into play in the composition and formation of the affects, and the mimetic mechanisms underpinning the combination of the gamut of actions and passions. Yet the primary triad of desire, joy and sadness never

---

[60] Ibid.: 'Each thing, in so far as it is simple and undivided, always remains in the same state, as far as it can.'

[61] *PP* II, 14; *CWS* I, 277.

[62] Cf. *Ethics* III, 6; *CWS* I, 498: 'Each thing, as far as it can by its own power, strives to persevere in its being.'

exists in isolation in raw form, but is always tied in a complex affective knot that fluctuates according to the situation. By virtue of its resolutive-compositive method, the *Ethics* shows the simplest elements and constructs a geometry of affects that does not give the full extent of their affective power within human societies, according to how they are organised and their political regime. But this is not the objective of the *Ethics*, so it may seem pointless to draw conclusions about the system's development.

The difference in the approaches used in the *Ethics* and in the *Political Treatise*, however, should not mask the growing power of the active dimension in Spinoza's philosophy. In this respect, the transition from a geometric model dealing with the affects in the *Ethics* to a physical model in the *Political Treatise* is doubtless a sign of a more dynamic conception of power. Instead of lines, surfaces and bodies, which served as a paradigm in the Preface to *Ethics* III, Spinoza substitutes bad weather, thunder and other atmospheric phenomena[63] and adopts the classic vocabulary evoking movement and the emotion of the soul for this purpose, since he designates the passions by the term *animi commotiones*.[64] Far from being a return to Descartes, it would appear that this formulation is evidence of the profound transformation of the geometric mechanism of power into dynamism that occurs over the course of Spinoza's writings.

The *Political Treatise*, however, does not reject earlier analyses, since it repeats the key features of the theory developed in the *Ethics* and expressly refers to it.[65] In this sense, it is a field of application and experimentation for the theory of affects developed in Part III, and is anchored in the foundation that we should now update.

---

[63] Cf. *TP* I, 4; *CWS* II, 508: 'So I've contemplated human affects – like love, hate, anger, envy, love of esteem, compassion and the other emotions – not as vices of human nature but as properties which pertain to it in the same way heat, cold, storms, thunder, etc., pertain to the nature of the air.'

[64] Ibid.

[65] Cf. *TP* I, 5; *CWS* II, 505–6 and *TP* II, 1; *CWS* II, 507.

4

The Definition of 'Affect' in *Ethics* III

The Change in Terminology and the Translation Problem

The innovative nature of Spinoza's theory is first expressed at the level of vocabulary through the substitution of the word '*affectus*' for '*emotio*' or '*passio*' to refer to affective movements in people. In Spinoza, the main concept is no longer emotion, but affect. This change in terminology, however, must not be understood as a sweeping innovation or as a radical rejection. On the one hand, the term *affectus* already appears in Descartes and refers to passion or emotion in its double psychophysiological dimension. This is what emerges from the Latin text of the *Principles of Philosophy*, particularly §190 in which Descartes tackles the affects of the soul (*animi affectibus*) as well as natural appetites, and first equates emotions, passions and affects,[1] then affects and passions.[2] On the other hand, the concept of emotion, although rare, is present in Spinoza, and it is synonymous with affect. Thus, in Part IV of the *Ethics*, he says that 'the true knowledge of good and evil arouses disturbances of the mind (*animi commotiones*)'.[3] Now, since the true knowledge of good and evil is defined as an

---

[1] *Principiorum philosophiae*, pars quarta, CXC, AT VIII, p. 316, 24–5: '. . . in quo consistunt omnes animi commotiones, sive pathemata, et affectus.'

[2] *Principiorum philosophiae*, pars quarta, CXC, AT VIII, p. 317, 24: '. . . quatenus sunt tantum, affectus, sive animi pathemata.'

[3] *Ethics* IV, 17 Schol.; CWS I, 554–5.

affect,[4] it is clear that the terms are interrelated and overlapping. Spinoza himself corroborates this conclusion by equating affects and emotions on several occasions, such as in Proposition 2 of *Ethics* V, where he refers to 'emotions, or affects' (*animi commotionem, seu affectum*); in the Scholium to Proposition 20 of *Ethics* V, where he maintains that 'when we compare the affects of one and the same man with each other, and find that he is affected, or moved (*affici sive moveri*) more by one affect than by another'; and in *Political Treatise*, I, 4, where he asserts that he has

> contemplated human affects (*humanos affectus*) like love, hate, anger, envy, love of esteem, compassion and the other emotions (*animi commotiones*) – not as vices of human nature, but as properties which pertain to it in the same way heat, cold, storms, thunder, etc.

Although there is no reason to pit *affectus* and *commotio* against each other, the broad use of the first term rather than the second serves to draw our attention to the originality of Spinoza's definition. Though he did not coin the word, Spinoza endows it with an original meaning. Traditionally, in fact, *adfectus* referred above all to a disposition, a mood among philosophers, particularly in Cicero in the *Tusculan Disputations*.[5] It was taken as a synonym for feeling[6] or passion. In addition, it was also used in medicine to refer to a disposition of the body, an affliction or an illness. Spinoza captures the two meanings of this term together in a concept that includes both a bodily affliction and a mental modification. Affect therefore concerns the body primarily, in that it can be modified by virtue of its nature or its parts. Its condition of possibility lies in the existence of a finite mode of extension whose highly composite nature makes it capable of being affected in a large number of ways, at the level of its parts as well as in its

---

[4] Cf. *Ethics* IV, 8; *CWS* I, 550: 'The knowledge of good and evil is nothing but an affect of Joy or Sadness, insofar as we are conscious of it.'

[5] Cf. V, 47: 'Further the disposition (*adfectus*) of the soul in a good man is praiseworthy.'

[6] This is the case, for example, in Ovid's *Metamorphoses*, VIII, 473. '[She] wavered betwixt opposing passions' (*Dubiis affectibus errat*).

entirety.[7] Affect is therefore based on a physics of the human body conceived as a complex individual.

It must be noted, however, that affects are not unique to humans, because they can also influence highly complex individuals such as animals or the body politic. Although their nature differs from human nature, animals are subject to affects, particularly the desire to procreate.[8] Similarly, the body politic is prey to affects such as fear, hope, the desire for vengeance and ambition.[9] Its power is determined by the common power of the multitude, 'led as if by one mind'.[10] Now,

> a multitude naturally agrees, and wishes to be led, as if by one mind, not because reason is guiding them, but because of some common affect (*ex communi aliquo affectu*) [. . .] they have a common hope, or fear, or a common desire to avenge some harm.[11]

It follows that the power of the body politic is defined above all by passional affects. The concept therefore applies to the state as well as to individual people and other complex living beings.

Affect means, however, that the mind, because it is a thinking thing, forms a concept of the affects of its body. It does not matter here whether the idea is adequate or not. Affect considered in its

---

[7] This is what emerges, in particular, from *Ethics* II, 13 Post. 1 and 3; *CWS* I, 462: 'The human Body is composed of a great many individuals of different natures, each of which is highly composite.' 'The individuals composing the human Body, and consequently, the human Body itself, are affected by external bodies in very many ways.'

[8] Cf. *Ethics* III, 57 Schol.; *CWS* I, 528–9: 'From this it follows that the affects of the animals (*affectus animalium*), which are called irrational (for after we know the origin of the Mind, we cannot in any way doubt that the lower animals feel things), differ from men's affects as much as their nature differs from human nature. Both the horse and the man are driven by a desire to procreate; but the one is driven by an equine desire, the other by a human desire.' Translation modified.

[9] This is what emerges, for example from *TP* III, 14; *CWS* II, 523, where Spinoza analyses the motives for making and breaking alliances between bodies politic, such as the fear of loss or hope of gain.

[10] *TP* III, 2; *CWS* II, 517.

[11] *TP* VI, 1; *CWS* II, 532.

mental reality covers confused ideas as well as adequate ones. It would not immediately be equated with a confused idea, as would be the case in the general definition of the affects, where it is exclusively a question of the passions. The idea in question here is a mode of thinking in general, which is adequate when the affect is an action and inadequate when it is a passion. Affect is a psychophysical reality. Understanding the affects is therefore simultaneously analysing humankind as a mode of the attribute of thought, as well as a mode of the attribute of extension. As it unites a bodily affection and a mental affection that modify the power of acting, the concept of *affectus* in Spinoza therefore has a meaning that does not completely overlap with the traditional meanings of the term 'passion'.

This results in a translation difficulty. For example, in French, the terms '*passion*' and '*sentiment*' [TN: 'feeling'] that are generally used to translate the Latin *affectus* are not suitable here. The term '*passion*' is inadequate, at least in the *Ethics*, since Spinoza himself admits to there being active affects.[12] It may potentially be legitimate when we

---

[12] This is what Bernard Pautrat observes in his French translation of the *Ethics* (Seuil, 1988), p. 9: 'Apart from the fact that "*passion*" must be reserved for *passio*, which comes up on several occasions, it is an attempt to forget that not every *affectus* is a passion.' ('*Outre que «passion» doit être réservé pour passio qui intervient à plusieurs reprises, c'est vouloir oublier que ce n'est pas tout affectus qui est une passion.*')

Such a problem does not exist in the English translations, which clearly distinguish *affectus* and *affectio* without equating affects with passions. Samuel Shirley, in his translation of the *Ethics* (Indianapolis: Hackett Publishing, 1992), chose the word 'emotion' for *affectus* and 'affection' for *affectio*. It is not wrong to translate *affectus* as 'emotion' because Spinoza equates the two concepts expressly in *Ethics* V, 2, but the disappearance of the word 'affect' is unfortunate. Edwin Curley, editor and translator of *The Collected Works of Spinoza* (Princeton: Princeton University Press, 2016), rightly preferred the word 'affect' for *affectus* and still used 'affection' for *affectio*. It is the same situation in *Ethics*, ed. and trans. G. H. R. Parkinson (Oxford: Oxford University Press, 2000). As far as Italian translations are concerned, Emilia Giancotti used 'affetto' for *affectus* and 'affezione' for *affectio* in *Etica*, (Roma Editore Riuniti, 1988); Paolo Cristofolini did the same in his Italian translation (Pisa: Edizioni ETS, 2010). In the Spanish translations, Vidal Peña García (Madrid: Editora Nacional, 1980) used 'afecto' for *affectus* and 'affeción' for *affectio*, as did Atilano Dominguez in *Ética demostrada según el orden geométrico* (Madrid: Editorial Trotta, 2000).

are only dealing with passive affects. That, moreover, is why, in his French translation of the *Political Treatise*, Pierre-François Moreau translates *affectus* as 'passion', noting that in the whole of the work 'it is never a question of active affections'.[13] Yet even in this case, the translation of *affectus* as 'passion' remains debatable. On the one hand, it results in a loss of meaning, since the etymological link uniting the nouns *affectus* and *affectio*, and attaching them to the verb *afficere*, no longer appears distinctly. On the other hand, the possibility of going from a passive to an active affect by forming a clear and distinct idea[14] seems less clear-cut, while using the same word, *affectus*, in both cases underscores it more.

The term 'sentiment' chosen by Roland Caillois in the Pléiade edition, and later used by Ferdinand Alquié, is more appropriate than 'passion'. Nevertheless, it also has a connotation of passivity or receptivity, which makes it impossible to render the some-times active nature of *affectus*. In addition, it does not place enough emphasis on the bodily affection implied by *affectus*, since it describes a disposition of the soul, referring to its effusions. *Sentiment* therefore continues to be somewhat subjective, which is not very compatible with Spinoza's determination to deal with affective life geometrically.[15] Caillois himself recognises that 'the word *sentiment* has a subjective nuance that *affectus* does not'.[16]

---

[13] '*Il n'est jamais question d'affections actives.*' TN I, 1, p. 187, in Moreau, Pierre-François *Traité politique* (éditions Réplique, 1979).

[14] Cf. *Ethics* V, 3; *CWS* I, 598.

[15] This is also what Bernard Pautrat highlights in his translation of the *Ethics* (Seuil, 1988), p. 9:

> The tireless repetition of '*sentiment*' ends up creating a lot of haze, whereas it should be a question of, here more than anywhere else, giving the object '*affectus*' the solidity of a mathematical object, so that it can be treated like lines, planes and bodies. And furthermore, if '*sentiment*' was indeed what the author wanted to say, we have reason to think that he would have chosen another Latin word, perhaps *sensus*, which is traditionally translated as '*sentiment*'. Lastly, we would have once again risked drowning in the effusion that the French word '*sentiment*' invites us to, had it turned out to be impossible to do otherwise.

[16] '*le mot « sentiment » a une nuance subjective que n'a pas affectus.*' Cf. Spinoza, *Œuvres complètes*, note 3, p. 411 (édition de la Pléiade), p. 1432.

That is why nowadays translators and commentators generally agree in rendering the Latin *affectus* as 'affect',[17] and unani-
mously criticise Charles Appuhn's French translation, which opts
for referring to two different things, *affectus* and *affectio*, with the
same word, *affection*, thus inadvertently introducing a great deal
of confusion. In his defence, it must be recognised that Appuhn
reconciles himself with great reluctance to his choice of discarding
the currently preferred solution in order to avoid a neologism. 'If
the word *affect* or *affet* (*Affect* in German), formed in a manner
analogous to *effet* [TN: 'effect'], had existed in the vocabulary, it
would have spared a great deal of hesitation, but I could not take
it upon myself to create it.'[18]

It is true that the word *affect* has the drawback of being anach-
ronistic, since it only appeared in the French language in 1951 in
the context of the vocabulary of psychoanalysis. Before that, it
did not exist as a noun. According to the *Dictionnaire du français
classique*, starting from the fourteenth century it is possible to
find traces of the verb *affecter*, derived from the Latin *affectare*,
which means to desire, to seek vigorously, to love, or adopt a
manner of being sincere or fake.[19] Then, in the fifteenth century,
there are occurrences of the verb *affecter*, from the Latin *affectus*,
which refer to the idea of touching and moving in the emotional
sense. Since 1452 *l'affective* as a noun has referred to the faculty

[17] This is the case for Bernard Pautrat and Robert Misrahi in their new translations of the *Ethics*, for Pierre Macherey in his *Introduction à la troisième
partie de l'Ethique, la vie affective* (PUF, 1995), and for Jean-Marie Beyssade
in his article '*Nostri Corporis Affectus*: Can an Affect in Spinoza Be "of the
Body"?' in Y. Yovel (ed.), *Desire and Affect: Spinoza as Psychologist* (New
York: Little Room Press, 1999), pp. 113–28.

[18] 'Si le mot *affect* ou *affet* (en allemand *Affect*) de formation analogue à
effet, eût existé dans le vocabulaire, bien des hésitations m'eussent été
épargnées, mais je ne pouvais prendre sur moi de le créer.' Cf. Notes in
the Garnier edition of the *Ethics*, 1906, ibid. by Bernard Pautrat in his
translation of the *Ethics* (Seuil, 1988), p. 9, and by Robert Misrahi, Note 1,
p. 404, in his translation of the *Ethics* (PUF, 1990).

[19] It is in this sense that Corneille uses this verb in his verse translation of
The Imitation of Christ, III, 5698: '*La grâce aime l'habit simple et sans orne-
ment, elle n'affecte point la mode.*' ('Grace prefers simple and unadorned
clothing, it does not affect any fashion.')

of affection, the heart; the adjective *affectif* [TN: masculine form] or *affective* [TN: feminine form], in the sense of being moving and touching, also appeared in the seventeenth century,[20] but the term *affect* as such did not. Nevertheless, despite its anachronism, we must translate *affectus* in French as *affect*, which has come into common usage, and is less jolting now than at the beginning of the twentieth century,[21] when Charles Appuhn had good reason to hesitate in using it. This word, in fact, makes it possible to avoid confusion, and to account for the new meaning of this concept encompassing both the physical and mental dimensions.

The Problem of the Two Definitions

It is possible, however, to question whether a mixed discourse revolving around the analysis of the affects really exists. The nature of this concept, indeed, appears problematic, since Spinoza proposes two definitions of it that are noticeably different, even divergent, from each other, the first in the beginning and the other at the end of Part III. The first brings together 'affections of the Body by which the Body's power of acting is increased or diminished, aided or constrained, and at the same time (*et simul*), the ideas of these affections'[22] under the term 'affect' and distinguishes two types – actions and passions. The second, presented as a general definition,[23] seems less bold than the first:

> An Affect that is called a Passion of the Mind is a confused idea, by which the Mind affirms of its Body, or of some part of it, a greater or lesser force of existing than before, which, when it is given, determines the Mind to think of this rather than that.

---

[20] There are, for example, traces of it in a text by Mme de Sévigné dated 5 June 1675: '*les paroles les plus répétées et les plus affectives qu'on puisse imaginer*' ('the most reiterated and affecting words that one can possibly imagine').

[21] A similar tendency can be observed in English translations. In the twentieth century, translators from Elwes to Shirley preferred using the word 'emotion' instead of 'affect' but, in the wake of Curley's translation, the term 'affect' has become the most common.

[22] *Ethics* III, Def. 3; CWS I, 493. Translation modified.

[23] *Ethics* III, General Definition of the Affects; CWS I, 542–3.

The final definition introduces three differences with respect to the previous one. First, it limits the affects to passions and does not mention actions. So the crux of the problem lies in determining the exact value and meaning of the expression '*qui animi pathema vocatur*',[24] which is ambiguous in Latin. It can, in fact, be interpreted in two ways, either as a statement of a strict equivalence between affects and passions of the mind, such that the two terms are rigorously synonymous and interchangeable, or as a statement of a particular determination indicating that here it is a question of only one type of affect, namely passions of the mind.

Regardless of the hypothesis chosen, difficulties arise. The first interpretation poses a problem with respect to the internal coherence of the system. If Spinoza equated affects exclusively with passions of the mind in the general definition, he would contradict his earlier analyses when he extended this concept to actions and violate the precepts of terminological rigour by creating confusion. The second interpretation, which postulates that the final definition concerns only a particular type of affect, namely passions, avoids the previous pitfall and preserves the concept's coherence while confirming its first meaning, which includes actions. However, it makes us go from Scylla to Charybdis, since in this case it is difficult to understand why this definition is called a general one.

Second, the final definition limits affects to only their mental aspect. Affect is presented as a passion *of the mind*,[25] and more precisely as 'a confused idea, by which the Mind affirms of its Body, or of some part of it, a greater or lesser force of existing than before'. By underscoring the affirmative nature of the idea, Spinoza implicitly introduces a reference to will, seeing that voli-

---

[24] This expression, rarely used by Spinoza, appears in Descartes' *Principles of Philosophy*: I, 48, AT VIII, 23; and IV, 190, AT VIII, 317, as Jean-Marie Beyssade has demonstrated. Cf. '*Nostri Corporis Affectus*: Can an Affect in Spinoza Be "of the Body"?' in Y. Yovel (ed.), *Desire and Affect: Spinoza as Psychologist*, p. 118. 'The expression *animi pathema*, unusual in Spinoza, appears in Descartes's *Principles of Philosophy*: in contrast to the intellectual or internal emotions, this expression refers to the passions of the mind and, as in Spinoza's closing definition, it is equivalent to "certain confused thoughts".' Cf. also note 16, p. 126.

[25] Emphasis added.

tion is nothing other than the affirmation or the negation that the idea involves.[26] He therefore defines 'affect' by placing it solely within the framework of the attribute of thought, since will refers to striving as it is related only to the mind.[27] Of course, this does not exclude all physical references, since the mind is presented as affirming its body's or a part of its body's greater or lesser force of existing than before. The general definition, nevertheless, inverts the order of analysis with respect to Definition 3 of the affects, which begins with the body and gives more precision to it. It favours the mental aspect, since the body is not mentioned for its own sake as a mode of extension, but as an object of a confused idea affirmed by the mind.

This restriction is not insignificant, since although Definition 3 presents the mind and the body on an equal footing and creates the possibility of a joint approach, the general definition, on the other hand, invites us above all to consider affect from a mental angle. Under these circumstances, what happens to the much-vaunted mixed discourse? Is it legitimate, in the light of the final definition, to make affect a central concept, making it possible to conceptualise the link between a mode of thought and a mode of extension and to shed light on the way in which they are connected?

Third, the general definition adds a crucial detail that makes it possible to cover all the primitive affects. By specifying that affect is a confused idea 'which, when it is given, determines the mind to think of this rather than that', it expresses not only the nature of joy or sadness, but also that of desire.[28] In a sense, it thus supplements Definition 3, which includes in its wording an increase or decrease in the power of acting, in other words, joy or sadness, but does not explicitly reveal the nature of desire.

Although the addition of this detail is hardly problematic,

---

[26] Cf. *Ethics* II, 49; CWS I, 484.

[27] Cf. *Ethics* III, 9 Schol.; CWS I, 500.

[28] Cf. General Definition of the Affects, Exp.; CWS I, 543: 'Finally, I added *which determines the Mind to think of this rather than that* in order to express also, in addition to the nature of Joy and Sadness (which the first part of the definition explains), the nature of Desire.'

inasmuch as it completes the previous definition without calling it fundamentally into question, the two restrictions do raise more questions, seeing that they touch upon the very nature of affect. The question that then arises concerns the respective statuses of these two definitions. Must they be put on an equal footing? Must we consider the first to be more conclusive by virtue of its more general scope, or, on the contrary, that the second is the definitive one by virtue of its final position?

In reality, the issue should not be framed in such terms, because it is obvious that Spinoza does not backpedal on the existence of active affects and that the general definition cannot be interpreted as an abandonment of his previous arguments. The last two propositions of *Ethics* III, which precede the final summary, attest to the contrary, since they introduce the affects called actions, and bring them together under the category of strength of character. The subsequent sections devoted to them in Parts IV and V definitively destroy the hypothesis of Spinoza's reversal on the subject.

It then remains to be seen why these active affects are eliminated from a definition that claims to be a general one. The adjective *generalis* leads to confusion, seeing that the definition is not universal. The ambiguity dissipates once we clarify the exact meaning of this expression. The apparent contradiction between Definition 3 and the final definition stems from the fact that the adjective 'general' is interpreted as targeting all the affects. Now, since this is not the case, the use of this qualifier seems inappropriate and requires explanation.

The hypothesis sometimes put forward to resolve this difficulty consists in considering the final definition as being written prior to certain texts from Part III of the *Ethics*. The final definition had not subsequently been revised and would therefore bear traces of previous conceptions, where Spinoza systematically equated affects and passions of the mind. Jonathan Bennet, for example, resorts to this type of explanation in order to account for the distortions between the different definitions of joy, which is identified, in turn, as a passion of the mind,[29] a human affect[30] and

---

[29] Cf. *Ethics* III, 11 Schol.; CWS I, 500–1.
[30] *Ethics* III, DA 2; CWS I, 531.

an action.[31] The remaining disparities are attributed to Spinoza's oversight. After changing his mind, he forgot to modify his text in certain places and update it in line with his new thought.[32]

This hypothesis is hardly acceptable. Even though certain passages of the summary text devoted to the definitions of the affects would have been written before the demonstrations that preceded them, it is obvious that Spinoza had reviewed the whole, since he refers almost systematically to propositions in Part III, and then modifies and clarifies them. As for the general definition, it appears, on the contrary, so clearly to come after Definition 3 that it seems difficult to accept that it is the residue of earlier concepts that had not been corrected. This is because it completes Definition 3 by including the nature of desire and all the primitive affects whereas, before, only joy and sadness had been emphasised. Consequently, if Spinoza had wanted to say that all affects are passions, he would have noticed and avoided the inconsistency between the last two propositions of *Ethics* III, which allow for active affects, and the general definition.

Of course, certain clues suggest that the text on the definitions of the affects reflects a state of thought that is more influenced by Cartesian analyses than are Demonstrations 1 to 59 of Part III. The final appendix could thus correspond to a moment when Spinoza situates his philosophy of the passions with respect to Descartes', in order to show how different he is from his authoritative predecessor and to justify his positions. In fact, it is interesting to note that the order of the affects listed at the end of Part III does not reproduce the order of deduction of the propositions, but partially follows Descartes' listing of the primitive passions and their derivatives[33] in the beginning.

---

[31] *Ethics* III, 58; CWS I, 529.

[32] *A Study of Spinoza's* Ethics, p. 258: 'It is pretty clear that at some stage in the development of his views Spinoza did think of all pleasure as passive, and that when he changed his mind about this he made an imperfect job of cleansing his text.'

[33] The seven first affects listed in Part III, in order, are: desire, joy, sadness, love, hate, sympathy and antipathy, followed by hope, fear, confidence, gladness and remorse, etc. The seven affects defined at the end, in order, are: desire, joy, sadness, wonder, disdain (*contemptus*), love and hate, followed

The expression '*affectus qui animi pathema dicitur*', which is clearly drawn from Descartes' *Principles of Philosophy*,[34] also gives credence to the idea that Spinoza positions himself with respect to his illustrious predecessor. The emphasis on the confused nature of passion, after all, is a feature found in the French philosopher's work. What is more, that is why Descartes believes it to be more exact to describe the passions as feelings rather than perceptions,[35] seeing that the latter can sometimes be clear and distinct while the former are often vague and always confused. Whether or not it is valid, this hypothesis of a contrast with Descartes cannot be invoked to support the argument of an affectivity that is exclusively passive and mental, since, for the author of the *Principles of Philosophy*, the term 'passion of the mind' is contrasted with intellectual emotions caused by only the mind and always entails an action of the body. Consequently, the differences between Spinoza's two definitions of the affects should not be interpreted as a disavowal of the active and corporeal nature of affects but, rather, that they must be due to other reasons.

In reality, the key to the problem lies in the status of the final text that Spinoza briefly introduces in the explanation of Definition 48:

If we wish now to attend to these primitive affects, and to what was said above about the nature of the Mind, we shall be able to

by inclination, aversion, devotion and mockery. It is clear that in the definitions of the affects, at first Spinoza positions himself critically with respect to Descartes' listing and his six primitive passions, since he mentions wonder (which is not an affect) in fourth position, whereas in Part III wonder is only mentioned belatedly in 52 Schol. The surprising presence of disdain (DA 5) in fifth place, while in Part III it only appears in 52 Schol., can thus be explained by its connection to wonder in Descartes. Indeed, contempt, with esteem, is the first particular passion derived from wonder (cf. *Passions of the Soul* LIV). Similarly, if Spinoza mentions veneration and contempt at the end of Definition 5 of the affects in order to justify his leaving them out, it is because these passions are also types of wonder in Descartes and, more precisely, forms of esteem and contempt for objects considered to be free causes capable of doing good and evil (cf. *Passions of the Soul* LIV).

[34] §190, cited above: '. . . *affectus sive animi pathemata*', AT VIII, 317, 24.
[35] *Passions of the Soul* I, XXVIII.

define the affects, insofar as they are related only to the Mind, as follows.

Before expounding on his statement, Spinoza thus clearly explains that his plan is not to define the affects in all their aspects but only as they are related to the mind (*quatenus ad solam mentem referentur*). This is why reference to the body is minimised, although it does not disappear completely. We still do not understand why Spinoza devotes himself above all to the mind on the one hand and to its passions on the other. This primacy does not mean that the body is excluded or that active affects have been eliminated. It is the consequence of the goal Spinoza explicitly aims to reach in the second Scholium to Proposition 56: 'For our purpose, which is to determine the powers of the affects and the power of the Mind over the affects, it is enough to have a general definition of each affect.' The general definition thus fits into the context of an investigation into how the power of the mind can moderate and constrain the affects. That is why he emphasises not only the mental but also the passive aspect of affects. It is a question of understanding the nature of the passions in order to measure their powers, and to be able to oppose them with the power of the intellect. The definitions of the affects taken as a whole thus have a pedagogical and introductory function. They draw attention to what we need to observe[36] with respect to the passions, in order then to be able to determine the causes of human bondage – in other words the powers of the affects in line with the title of Part IV, their good or bad nature, as well as the road to freedom in Part V, using the power of the intellect.[37]

---

[36] This is the term Spinoza uses in *Ethics* III, 59 Schol.; CWS I, 528: 'Finally, there are certain things to be noted about the definitions of the affects. I shall therefore repeat them here in order, interposing the observation required on each one.'

[37] This is what Emilia Giancotti suggests after noting the difference between the two definitions of the affects, and the elimination of active affects in the latter definition: 'The reason for this change – or rather this elimination – is not clear, since the double condition of agent and patient cannot be eliminated from human nature. Perhaps, as he prepares to go on to treat human bondage, Spinoza wishes to stress the condition of passivity,

Under these circumstances, the definition is called 'general' because it is generic; it refers to a genus of affect, namely passions, or confused ideas by which the mind affirms of its body a greater or lesser force of existing than before. It does not exclude the existence of another genus of affect, or actions that bring together adequate ideas by which the mind affirms of its body a greater force of existing than before. The adjective '*generalis*' must therefore be understood through reference to genus. The use of this concept with respect to affects is not inappropriate, and is not an extrapolation, since Spinoza himself applies this name to them. This is what emerges, for example, from Definition 5 of *Ethics* V:

> By opposite affects I shall understand, in what follows, those which pull a man in different directions, although they are of the same *genus* (*quamvis eusdem sint generis*) – such as gluttony and greed, which are species of love, and are opposite, not by nature but accidentally.[38]

The classification by genus and species is governed by the search for a common standard among diverse individuals in order to be able to compare them. It leaves out their distinctive features in order to bring them to a common, general property. At least, this is how Spinoza accounts for the formation of the idea of genus in the Preface to *Ethics* IV, in the explanation of the origin of the concepts of perfection and imperfection:

> We are accustomed to refer all individuals in Nature to one genus, which is called the most general, that is, to the notion

which is the basis of bondage.' 'The Theory of the Affects in the Strategy of Spinoza's *Ethics*', in *Desire and Affect: Spinoza as Psychologist*, p. 131.

This is also the opinion of Jean-Marie Beyssade, for whom the positioning of the general definition of the affects in favour of the passions is perfectly understandable and justified. This becomes clear when taking into account Spinoza's two objectives in Parts IV and V, namely, to analyse bondage, or the powers of the affects, and freedom, by taking the point of view of the mind, of the power of the intellect. It would also be legitimate, however, to take the perspective of the body in other disciplines, such as medicine. Cf. '*Nostri Corporis Affectus*: Can an Affect in Spinoza Be "of the Body"?' in Y. Yovel (ed.), *Desire and Affect: Spinoza as Psychologist*, p. 119.

[38] Translation modified.

of being, which pertains absolutely to all individuals in Nature. So insofar as we refer all individuals in Nature to this genus, compare them to one another, and find that some have more being, or reality, than others, we say that some are more perfect than others.

This operation then makes it possible to compare individuals and categorise them from imperfect to more perfect, depending on their degree of being or reality.

It would appear that the final definition of the affects is governed by the same concern. It is called 'general' because it relates all the passions to a single genus, the confused idea, and then makes it possible to compare them according to their ability to increase or decrease humanity's power of acting. The use of the notion of genus is intended to categorise and assess the affects according to whether they are used for good or evil. It foreshadows the plan that will be carried out immediately afterwards in *Ethics* IV, where Spinoza intends not only to explain the causes of bondage but also 'what there is of good and evil in the affects'.[39]

The interest in reducing the affects to genera is to avoid extraneous steps, in line with the third precept of the method instructing us to 'establish an order, so that we do not become weary with trifles'.[40] Spinoza is explicitly agreeing with this point of view:

> For our purpose, which is to determine the powers of the affects and the power of the Mind over the affects, it is enough to have a general definition of each affect. It is enough, I say, for us to understand the common properties of the affects.[41]

The general definition is equated here with displaying the common properties of the affects, rather than analysing their distinctive features in detail or taking an inventory of each particular case. By confining the investigation to a general definition, Spinoza advises us to restrict ourselves to the second kind of

---

[39] *Ethics* IV, Praef.; CWS I, 543.
[40] Cf. *TdIE* 49; CWS I, 22.
[41] *Ethics* III, 56 Schol.; CWS I, 527.

knowledge of the affects – since he aims to identify their common characteristics – and not to determine the particular features of each on the basis of the idea of the essence of the attributes of extension and thought. The adjective *generalis* therefore indicates that we are dealing with a rational, rather than an intuitive, definition of the affects.

This observation is valid for all the definitions of the affects, which provide a review of Part III. Their principles are based on a knowledge of the second type, and are governed by the need to identify the main features common to all desires, joys, sadnesses, loves and hates, without being weighed down with all their species and possible names. It is doubtless why Definition 1 of desire is very broad and includes 'all the strivings of human nature that we signify by the name of appetite, will, desire, or impulse', even though these concepts had been differentiated in the Scholium to Proposition 9 in Part III, and the term *cupiditas* may take on a more specific and circumscribed meaning in other contexts.

A question, however, remains unanswered: why is a general definition sufficient, and why is it not necessary to go further, into the specific details of each affect? Does Spinoza not tell us himself that knowledge of the third kind is preferable to the second kind because it affects us more?[42] Consequently, if the active affects generated by intuitive knowledge are more powerful than those arising from reason, they represent more effective weapons to constrain the passive affects. It therefore seems strange to attempt to do without them.

To resolve this paradox, we must refer to the justifications Spinoza provides in order to explain why he limits himself to general knowledge and omits the definition of certain particular affects:

I pass over in silence the definitions of Jealousy and the other vacillations of mind, both because they arise from the composition of affects we have already defined, and because most of them do not have names. This shows that it is sufficient for practical purposes to know them only in general (*easdem in*

---

[42] *Ethics* V, 36 Schol.; CWS I, 612–13.

genere tantummodo noscere). Furthermore, from the definitions of the affects we have explained, it is clear that they all arise from Desire, Joy or Sadness or, rather, that they are nothing but these three, each one generally called by a different name on account of its varying relations and extrinsic denominations.[43]

Spinoza puts forward three main reasons that all aim to show the pointlessness of a specific analysis of each affect. The first two legitimise above all the omission of the definitions of jealousy and other vacillations of mind, while the other takes on a more general scope and applies to all affects. First, the definition of jealousy and other vacillations of mind is superfluous, because their nature is included in the affects that have already been defined, such as love, hate and *fluctuatio animi*, because it results from their composition. Thus, jealousy 'is nothing but a vacillation of mind born of Love and Hatred together, accompanied by the idea of another who is envied'.[44] Second, apart from the composite nature that makes them simple variations of affects previously defined, certain passions do not warrant spending too much time on them by virtue of how insignificant they are in terms of their usefulness in life. It is therefore a question of only considering affects that are important to us, to the extent that we feel the need to name them and identify them distinctly. The study of the nature of the affects is not an end in itself; it is, rather, a means of achieving beatitude. That is why it is not a question of deducing everything, but of only selecting that which 'can lead us, by the hand, as it were, to the knowledge of the human Mind and its highest beatitude',[45] as the Preface to *Ethics* II instructs us. Usefulness in life serves as the principle of discrimination between the affects worthy of being named and defined and those that can be neglected. From this perspective, Spinoza remains very close to Descartes, for whom it was a question of carrying out a sufficient and non-exhaustive enumeration of the passions of the soul. Indeed, Descartes does not intend to inventory all the ways in which objects affect us and

---

[43] *Ethics* III, DA 48 Exp.; CWS I, 541–2.
[44] *Ethics* III, 35 Schol.; CWS I, 514.
[45] Translation modified.

all the effects they can produce in us, just those that are important to us, which can harm or benefit us.[46] The passions are categorised and analysed according to whether they are useful or harmful. Similarly, it is not at all important to Spinoza to define and enumerate all the species of affect, since this is not necessary for living and living well. Usefulness in life is a criterion that makes it possible to justify the sufficiency of a general definition.

But the third argument, the decisive one, remains the fact that all the particular passions do not need to be defined because they are composed from the three primitive affects, and only represent ways of naming desire, joy and sadness differently on account of their varying relationships. Under these circumstances, it is enough for the general definition of the affects to express the nature of joy, sadness and desire for all passions to be included in it and for them to be deduced from it. This is why the possibility of a general definition of the passion of the mind is based on considering not only the nature of the mind but also the nature of the three primitive affects. Indeed, Spinoza underscores this point:

> If we wish now to attend to these primitive affects, and to what was said above about the nature of the Mind, we shall be able to define the affects, insofar as they are related only to the Mind, as follows.[47]

The general definition indeed confirms these two conditions. First, it is based on knowledge of the nature of the mind, since it is presented here as an idea affirming the body's force of existing, and its inadequate causality, since passion is a confused idea. Second, it includes the nature of joy and sadness, since it specifies that the mind 'affirms of its Body, or of some part of it, a greater or lesser force of existing than before', as well as that of desire, since it adds that the presence of this confused idea 'influences the Mind to think of this rather than that'.

Ultimately, although the passions are emphasised, this does not

---

[46] *Passions of the Soul* II, LII.
[47] *Ethics* III, DA 48 Exp.; CWS I, 542.

mean that Spinoza contradicts himself or that the text of the definition of the affects necessarily came before and is therefore evidence of thought that was still incomplete on the issue. Rather, it
means that it is important above all to pay attention to the general
characteristics of the affects in order to be able to determine their
powers, their usefulness or harmfulness, and the power of the mind
to moderate or constrain them. In the end, the general definition
teaches us three main lessons.

First, Spinoza's ethics undertaking can and must, under certain
conditions, only call upon knowledge of the second kind, since
it is useless to wear out the intellect with the search for an intuitive knowledge of all the affects. Knowledge of the third kind is
certainly superior to the second, but it is not systematically preferable and does not necessarily represent progress in all cases. By
recommending that we limit ourselves to general definitions of the
affects, Spinoza draws the contours of a sphere of extension and
validity specific to knowledge of the second kind. Of course, this
does not prohibit us from seeking intuitive understanding but this
approach may merely be pointless curiosity, since human beings
have limited powers. Usefulness in life does not require a useless
expenditure of powers insofar as we recognise the effectiveness of
knowledge through reason. The general definition illustrates this
principle of saving effort that underlies Spinoza's philosophy. It
expresses the power of reason, which does not much care for intu-
ition under certain conditions.

Second, the general definition provides information about the
nature of the mixed discourse and its diverse variations. Far from
taking the form of a strict parallelism between the mind and the
body, it expresses an asymmetry – because the mental aspect
prevails over the physical and invites us to question not only
the alternating points of view under which humanity is analysed
but also the respective weight of the mode of extension and the
mode of thought in the formation of affects, according to their
genus and their active or passive nature.

Third, by dealing only with the passions of the mind, the
general definition is paradoxically only a particular case of
Definition 3, and legitimises it in its own right. At most, the general definition confirms and completes Definition 3 but does not

invalidate it, such that Definition 3 must fundamentally underpin the examination of the essence of the affects.

The Nature of the Affects According to Definition 3

By associating certain physical affections and their ideas, Definition 3 of the affects does not limit itself to the mental aspect. Instead, it involves capturing the mind and the body together (*simul*). Spinoza formulates it in two steps: he begins by elucidating the essence of affects in general, then he subdivides them into two broad categories, actions and passions, depending on whether the cause is adequate or inadequate. But regardless of whether they are active or passive, affects have two sides, a physical as well as mental one. That is why it is necessary to analyse their corporeal and mental aspects in turn, and determine how they are linked. Indeed, understanding the nature of affects involves clarifying the meaning of the expression '*et simul*', which links the affections of the body with the ideas of these affections in Definition 3. What exactly does Spinoza mean when he maintains that by 'affect' he understands 'affections of the body by which the body's power of acting is increased or diminished, aided or constrained, and *at the same time*,[48] the ideas of these affections'? It is clear, as Bernard Rousset[49] points out, that the essence of the affect depends on the semantic value of the adverb '*simul*' and that the examination of its meaning is of great interest, since it would shed light on the nature of the mixed discourse.

The Corporeal Aspect of Affect

Whatever its form, it must be noted that affect is defined, first, with respect to the body. It has physical affection as a necessary condition, and it must be understood first by reference to the attribute of extension. This priority given to the body is fully in line with the nature of the mind. If the mind is nothing other than the idea of the body and of its affections, everything that

---

[48] Emphasis added. Translation modified.
[49] Cf. Olivier Bloch (ed.), *Spinoza au XXe Siècle* (PUF, 1993), p. 141.

happens in it is a function of its object. In that case, we must know beforehand what is affecting the body in order to understand what is affecting the mind. In Definition 3 Spinoza thus rigorously complies with the conditions of possibility of knowledge of the human mind and its power, which he had formulated in the Scholium to Proposition 13 in *Ethics* II.[50] Equality, consequently, does not exclude priority, and is based here on the primacy of the body, for it is true that an idea cannot exist without an object.

Nevertheless, we must not believe that the place given to the body in Definition 3 is evidence of favouring the mode of extension, and that the mode of thought's role is limited to recording and reflecting physical changes, for it is true that the mind expresses its own power by forming ideas that cannot be reduced to 'something mute, like a picture on a tablet'.[51] On the one hand, the final definition of the affects demonstrates the reversibility of the order of priority, by underscoring the mental dimension of affect. On the other hand, the distinction at the end of Definition 3 between the two categories of affects, actions and passions, invites us to temper our propensity to hypostasise the physical dimension, since it is evidence of the primacy of the mind[52] and of reference to the attribute of thought.

The difference between action and passion lies, in fact, in the adequate or inadequate nature of the cause producing the affection: 'therefore, if we can be the adequate cause of any of these affections, I understand by the affect an action; otherwise, a passion.' We are an adequate cause when we produce an effect that our nature alone understands clearly and distinctly. By contrast, we are an inadequate cause when the effect is not intelligible solely by our nature and requires us to refer to external factors.[53] The division of the affects into two genera is thus based on a

---

[50] 'To determine the difference between the human mind and the others, and how it surpasses them, it is necessary for us, as we have said, to know the nature of its object, that is, of the human body.'

[51] *Ethics* II, 43 Schol.; CWS I, 479.

[52] This is what Michael Schrijvers notes in 'The Conatus and the Mutual Relationship Between Active and Passive Affects in Spinoza', in Y. Yovel (ed.), *Desire and Affect: Spinoza as Psychologist*, p. 63.

[53] Cf. *Ethics* III, Def. 1; CWS I, 492.

mode of thinking, namely the adequate or inadequate nature of the cause. Even if the concepts of action and passion apply to the body, the fact remains that the criteria differentiating them is above all intellectual and presupposes an aptitude of the mind to conceive the cause, on the one hand, and, on the other, to verify whether its effect is intelligible by the mind alone. Far from corroborating the idea of the radical primacy of the body in Definition 3, the distinction between actions and passions falls under the attribute of thought, since it involves the possibility of clearly and distinctly perceiving the effect as completely or partially contained in the cause. Furthermore, Spinoza underscores the correlation between the nature of the affect and the nature of the idea. In Proposition 3, he maintains that 'the actions of the Mind arise from adequate ideas alone; the passions depend on inadequate ideas alone'. Therefore Definition 3 first emphasises the role of the body and the modifications of its power of acting before referring to the mind, in order to divide the emotions into categories.

Affects and Affections

But if affect first refers to a bodily affection, does this mean that these two concepts overlap perfectly and that there is no difference between them? Unlike affect, the term 'affection' is not properly defined. Nevertheless, Spinoza makes the nature and meaning of this concept explicit in his final analysis of desire:

> For by an affection of the human essence we understand any constitution (*constitutionem*) of that essence, whether it is innate [NS: or has come from outside], whether it is conceived through the attribute of Thought alone, or through the attribute of Extension alone, or is referred to both at once.'[54]

The affection of the human essence in general therefore refers either to a mental state that is explained with reference to thought, to a physical state that is explained with respect to extension, or

[54] *Ethics* III, DA 1 Exp.; CWS I, 531.

to a psychophysical state that is explained with respect to the two attributes. These states are innate or acquired, and refer to both a given constitution and to its modifications over time. The scope of the concept of affection is therefore broad, since it not only covers every state, whether or not it is innate, but also all human reality and its diverse modes of understanding. Affection does not just concern the body alone; it also concerns the mind alone, or even the mind and body taken together. Thus, for example, trembling, paleness, tears and laughter are affections related to the body alone, and this, incidentally, is why Spinoza does not spend too much time on their analysis.[55] Imagining a particular thing, on the other hand, is an affection of the mind.[56] One and the same affection may, depending on the case, be the subject of a single, double or even triple conception, and take on different names depending on whether it refers to the body alone, the mind alone or both at once. This is the case with appetite, decisions of the mind and determinations of the body, which

> by nature exist together – or, rather, are one and the same thing, which we call a decision when it is considered under, and explained through, the attribute of Thought, and which we call a determination when it is considered under the attribute of Extension and deduced from the laws of motion and rest.[57]

The human appetite is a psychophysical reality involving a relationship with both mind and body, and cannot be explained without referring to both. It is, in fact, nothing other than 'the very essence of man, insofar as it is determined to do what promotes his preservation'.[58] Although affection includes any and

---

[55] *Ethics* III, 59 Schol.; CWS I, 530. 'As for the external affections of the Body, which are observed in the affects – such as trembling, paleness, sobbing, laughter, and the like – I have neglected them, because they are related to the Body only, without any relation to the Mind.'

[56] Cf. *Ethics* III, 52 Schol.; CWS I, 523. 'This affection of the Mind, or this imagination of a singular thing, insofar as it is alone in the Mind, is called Wonder.'

[57] *Ethics* III, 2 Schol.; CWS I, 497.

[58] *Ethics* III, DA 1 Exp.; CWS I, 531.

all innate or acquired states of essence, appetite appears in the category of innate affections. Though it can change over time, it is by nature an innate affection of the human essence, a given state, which makes human beings act with a view to their self-preservation. It boils down to the *conatus*, the effort to persevere in being, which 'is nothing but the given, or actual, essence of the thing itself'. But although the two concepts are synonymous, appetite refers more specifically to the effort to persevere in being, insofar as it is related to both mind and body,[59] and therefore involves the reference to both thought and extension. The same affection, called appetite, can be explained in purely physical terms and is related solely to the body and extension. In this case, we will no longer speak in terms of appetites but of determinations. Lastly, it can be considered in purely mental terms and relate to the mind alone, in which case we will talk instead in terms of decisions. These three explanations are not contradictory, since they are distinct but mutually consistent ways of conceptualising the same thing.

The question then arises about whether it is possible to apply what is valid for affections to affects, and to distinguish between physical, mental and psychophysical affects. In order to avoid drawing hasty conclusions, we must first note that an affection of the body is a necessary but not sufficient condition for the formation of an affect. Indeed, Spinoza restricts the definition of the concept of affect to only 'affections of the Body by which the Body's power of acting is increased or diminished, aided or constrained'[60] and to 'the ideas of these affections'. In other words, all affects are affections, but not all affections are affects. Thus, for example, the wonder felt by the mind, which remains fixed in the imagination of a new thing, involves an affection of the body and an idea of this affection, but it is not an affect for all that. Spinoza recognises that wonder is an affection[61] but he does not count it

---

[59] *Ethics* III, 9 Schol.; *CWS* I, 500.
[60] Translation modified.
[61] *Ethics* III, 52 Schol.; *CWS* I, 523: 'This affection of the Mind, or this imagination of a singular thing, insofar as it is alone in the Mind, is called Wonder.'

among the affects. Given that it comes down to imagining a new thing, it is indistinguishable by nature from other modes of imagining; and this is why the author of the *Ethics* maintains that, as far as he is concerned, he 'do[es] not number Wonder among the affects'.[62]

Spinoza thus differentiates himself from Descartes, not only by excluding wonder but because he restricts the domain of the affects only to affections that increase or decrease, aid or constrain the power of acting. In Descartes, by contrast, the passions of the soul or the actions of the body include everything that takes place or occurs, and they are identified with change in general, whatever its form.[63] It is true that in his enumeration of the passions, Descartes considers only the emotions objects arouse in us, not 'because of differences in the objects, but only because of the various ways in which they may harm or benefit us'.[64] He does not inventory all the affections, but only those involving our self-preservation. The difference between the two authors is therefore less marked than it would appear.

Nonetheless, in Definition 3, Spinoza splits affections into those that are affects and those that are not. Only four types of bodily affections, categorised by pairs of opposites and their ideas, can be called affects: those that increase the body's power of acting, those that diminish it, those that aid it, and those that constrain it. Before going into an analysis of this typology, it is important to understand why all the bodily affections do not systematically produce affects and to determine whether there is an obvious impossibility here. The reason for this division within the affections stems from the nature of the human body and its ability to act and be acted upon in a great many ways. This is what emerges from Postulate 1 of *Ethics* III: 'The human Body can be affected in many ways in which its power of acting is increased or diminished,

---

[62] *Ethics* III, DA 4 Exp.; CWS I, 532.

[63] Cf. *Passions of the Soul* I, I: 'I note that whatever takes place or occurs is generally called by philosophers a "passion" with regard to the subject to which it happens and an "action" with regard to that which makes it happen.'

[64] *Passions of the Soul* II, LII.

and also in others which render its power of acting neither greater nor less.'[65] Spinoza therefore sorts the affections according to their impact on the body's power of acting. To justify this axiom, he explicitly builds on Postulate 1 and Lemmas 5 and 7, which follow Proposition 13 of Part II. The reference to Postulate 1 makes it possible to understand that the body's ability to be affected in ways that increase or diminish its power of acting – as well as in ways that do not increase or diminish it – is linked to the fact that it 'is composed of a great many individuals of different natures, each of which is highly composite'. Its great complexity therefore explains that the human body is predisposed to an indefinite multiplicity of states, from the most to the least favourable to its power of acting, with more neutral or indifferent states in the middle. The two Lemmas, 5 and 7, corroborate this analysis, by specifying the limits of this capability of being affected and by defining its scope. From the moment when the relationship of movement and rest existing between its parts is preserved, the individual lends itself to a very large number of modifications, such as the size of its parts (Lemma 5) or of its movement (Lemma 7), all the while retaining its nature. The body can, as a result, go through any state, provided that its form is preserved. The existence of affections that neither increase nor diminish the power of acting is therefore all the more possible since they do not compromise the power of acting in anything and do not threaten its bodily form in any way. What is more, Lemma 7 indirectly offers examples of affections that are not affects:

> Furthermore, the Individual so composed retains its nature, whether it is a whole, moves or is at rest, or whether it moves in this or that direction, so long as each part retains its motion, and communicates it, as before, to the others.

Thus, turning my gaze in the direction of my feet without any particular intention involves an affection of the body and an idea of this affection, but it is not necessarily an affect, since this gesture has no effect on my power of acting. This example, however,

---

[65] *Ethics* III, Post. 1; *CWS* I, 493.

shows that the line between affection and affect is a fine one, because it is enough that I carry out the same action intentionally in preparation for removing a splinter from my foot for it to increase my power of acting, and for it to transform *ipso facto* into an affect.

Under these circumstances, it is possible to ask whether ultimately all affections are likely to become affects in Spinoza. The case of wonder is enlightening in this respect, because although it is presented as a simple affection, it can nevertheless give rise to affects and participate in their formation. He defines the affect of devotion, for example, as 'a Love of one whom we wonder at'.[66] There is therefore a transition from affection to affect, such that the border between the two is not cut and dried. Sometimes Spinoza even indirectly equates the two, since he defines not only the affection but also the affect as a constitution (*constitutio*). In the demonstration of Proposition 18 in *Ethics* III, it is indeed a question of 'the constitution of the Body, or affect, (*corporis constitutio, seu affectus*)', as Jean-Marie Beyssade[67] points out.

This coincidence is no accident, since it is clear that all affections of the body and all ideas of these affections are affects, once they are adequately understood. A neutral modification that is the subject of true knowledge increases my power of thinking and consequently fills me with joy. In theory, any affection, such as wonder, for example, once it is known, strengthens my power of acting and legitimately becomes an affect of joy, or more exactly of gladness (*gaudium*), as it makes me feel my own virtue. This, at least, is what Spinoza suggests in the Scholium to *Ethics* V, 10:

> One, therefore, who is anxious to moderate his affects and appetites from the love of Freedom alone will strive, as far as he can, to come to know the virtues and their causes, and to fill his mind with the gladness (*animum gaudio*) which arises from the true knowledge of them.

---

[66] *Ethics* III, DA 10; CWS I, 533.
[67] Cf. '*Nostri Corporis Affectus*: Can an Affect in Spinoza Be "of the Body"?' in Y. Yovel (ed.), *Desire and Affect: Spinoza as Psychologist*, p. 121.

Now, since 'there is no affection of the Body of which we cannot form a clear and distinct concept',[68] it is evident that, by nature, any affection can, one way or another, become a joyous affect.[69] It is therefore possible to obtain gladness not only from knowledge of sad affects but from any affection or appetite.

However, before it is known adequately or used for beneficial or harmful ends, an affection is an affect if and only if it has an impact on the body's power of acting. The key concept that makes it possible to define the nature and the sphere of extension of affect is the body's *potentia agendi*. Affect does not have an absolute and independent existence separate from the power of acting; it is not only related to a cause and its effect but it also describes a particular type of effect.

The Nature of the Body's Power of Acting

But what is the body's power of acting? Michael Schrivjers notes that Spinoza's definition of the affects is confusing, particularly because he does not explain the meaning of his concept of the power of acting, so it is ambiguous.[70] Indeed, *agere* in Spinoza has

---

[68] *Ethics* V, 4; *CWS* I, 598.

[69] I completely agree with Jean-Marie Beyssade's conclusions on this subject: 'Every affection of the body is *de jure* an affect.' Ibid., p. 123.

[70] Cf. 'The *Conatus* and the Mutual Relationship Between Active and Passive Affects in Spinoza', in Y. Yovel (ed.), *Desire and Affect: Spinoza as Psychologist*, pp. 64–5: 'The first confusion lies in the notion of the "power of acting" itself. It is nowhere defined. What is the meaning of "acting"? Spinoza employs this term as parallel to the broad and logical sense of "following" (*sequi*), that is, in the sense of the sequence that connects effects to their causes. Thus, in EIp36, he affirms that from every existing thing must follow this or that effect. Existing things are acting things. This broad sense of the term "acting" is specified in EIIIdef2 as either a sequence in which an effect follows completely from a cause or a sequence in which the effect follows partially or incompletely. The difficulty here is that the complete and adequate case is also referred to by the term "to act" (in EIIIdef2), so that the same term has both a general and a particular meaning. Similarly, when one reads "power of acting" in EIIIdef3, one cannot know whether it refers to "acting" in a more general sense or to "acting" in an adequate manner.'

both a more general and a more specific meaning. It is first used more broadly with *sequi*, or that which follows from the cause. Acting means producing effects, by being either a complete or a partial cause. In this case, the power of acting includes actions as well as passions. *Agere*, in its more specific meaning, as stated in Definition 2 of *Ethics* III, means producing effects of which we are the adequate cause. In this case, the power of acting refers only to actions. *Agere* in Spinoza therefore has a broader sense than *actio*.

This double meaning, however, is not a sign of negligence or confusion. It is fully in line with the ontological status of the modes and makes it possible to express it. If, for God, acting means always producing actions, the same does not go for humans, who have to form them with external causes that are as likely to strengthen as to constrain their efforts. The power of acting of a thing refers to its perfection, its reality. That is why affect is often defined with respect to the concept of perfection, as affect has an impact on perfection, as is the case, for example, with joy and sadness. The concept of *potentia agendi* expresses the necessity inherent in the nature of things to produce effects. All things are determined from the necessity of the divine nature to exist and operate in a certain manner.[71] Thus, in line with Proposition 36 of Part I: 'Nothing exists from whose nature some effect does not follow.' The power of acting is the expression of this causal necessity of essence and of its determination to do everything that follows from its nature. It is defined as a force of existing, a *vis existendi*.[72]

But this force of existing takes the form of striving in finite modes, since it asserts itself by resisting the pressure of external causes. The power of a thing is then identical to its *conatus*,[73] its effort to persevere in its being, and to its actual or given essence. Under these circumstances it cannot be defined in isolation because it is enmeshed in nature and modified by external causes.

[71] Cf. *Ethics* I, 29; CWS I, 433.

[72] Spinoza explicitly equates the two concepts in *Ethics* III, in the General Definition of the Affects, Exp.; CWS I, 542: about the body, he states that 'its power of acting, or force of existing, is increased or diminished, aided or constrained'. Translation modified.

[73] Cf. *Ethics* III, 7 Dem.; CWS I, 499: 'the power of each thing, or the striving [. . .], the power, or striving, by which it strives to persevere in its being.'

This is why it is not only considered with respect to the internal necessity of its essence, but also to that of other things that concur with it. That is what is revealed in Proposition 7 of *Ethics* III, where 'the power of each thing' is equated in the demonstration with 'the striving by which it (*either alone or with others*)[74] does anything, or strives to do anything'. The power of acting therefore is nothing other than the perfection or the reality of a thing, taking into account the various modifications it undergoes when in contact with surrounding modes. It encompasses actions as well as passions, and necessarily involves reference to external causes. Thus, the power of the passions is not measured against our power but against the power of an external cause compared with our own.[75]

Spinoza, however, makes a distinction between the power of acting, which covers actions as well as passions, and the 'true power of acting', which only includes actions. This is what emerges from Proposition 52 of *Ethics* IV: 'but man's true power of acting, or virtue, is reason itself'. The true power of acting is therefore based, as its name indicates, on adequate knowledge; it excludes passions and is identical to virtue, as Definition 8 of *Ethics* IV highlights. 'By virtue and power I understand the same thing, that is (by III, 7), virtue, insofar as it is related to man, is the very essence, or nature, of man, to the extent that he has the power of bringing about certain things, which can be understood through the laws of his nature alone.' The true power of acting refers to that which falls under the laws of our nature alone. That is why 'no man desires that there be predicated of him any power of acting, or (what is the same) virtue, which is peculiar to another's nature and alien to his own'.[76]

So where does this leave the body's power of acting in particular? Spinoza analyses it correlatively with the mind's in the

---

[74] Emphasis added.
[75] Cf. *Ethics* IV, 5; CWS I, 549: 'The force and growth of any passion, and its perseverance in existing, are not defined by the power by which we strive to persevere in existing, but by the power of an external cause compared with our own.'
[76] *Ethics* III, 55 Cor. 2, Dem.; CWS I, 526.

Scholium to Proposition 13 in *Ethics* II, and determines it on the basis of two criteria that implicitly reproduce the distinction between the 'power of acting' and the 'true power of acting':

> I say this in general, that in proportion as a Body is more capable than others of doing many things at once, or being acted on in many ways at once, so its Mind is more capable than others of perceiving many things at once. And in proportion as the actions of a body depend more on itself alone, and as other bodies concur with it less in acting, so its mind is more capable of understanding distinctly.

The power of acting is first presented as being capable of acting and being acted upon in many ways at once. It therefore includes effects of which the body is an adequate and complete cause, as well as those of which it is an inadequate and partial cause. It must be noted that the ability to be acted upon appears among the criteria that make it possible to determine how one body prevails over another and contains more reality. Passivity is therefore not by nature marred by negativity, since a body that can be acted upon in various ways is more capable than a body that can be acted upon in only a few ways. Passivity is always a partial activity because, although it is an inadequate cause, the body nevertheless contributes to the production of affects with the aid of external causes. This is why it is incorporated in the power of acting. Therefore, actions and passions are not opposites. The crux of the problem is increasing the active part of the body in the production of affects. That is why its power is measured in proportion to the activity that participates in the formation of a thing.

The second criterion determining the power of acting is thus the greater or lesser ability to produce effects that depend on the body alone, without the aid of external causes. The more the body is the adequate cause, the greater is this capability. Now, if we believe Postulates 3 and 6, which follow Proposition 13 of *Ethics* II, the human body's power of acting expresses itself essentially through its ability to be affected in many ways by external bodies, and affecting them by moving and disposing them in a great many ways. That is why understanding the power of acting and measuring its extension necessarily entails understanding the affects and their powers.

Affect, in fact, tells the story of the *potentia agendi* and describes how it is modified, either because it affirms the consequences contained in the essence of the thing or because it varies, taking into account the constitution of the body, external causes, the resistance it encounters and the aid it is given. The realm of the affects encompasses all the variations of this power, the shifts and transitions between the affirmation of a greater or lesser reality. Affect, particularly when it is a passion, expresses the difference between a power of acting, taken as a capability, and its current existence, inasmuch as it covers a negation, seeing that humanity is only a part of nature. It expresses the differential relationship between God as he constitutes our mind and God as he constitutes the nature of other things. This issue of the power of acting takes on four principal forms, which will now be examined in greater detail to the extent that they make it possible to define the realm of affect, and to distinguish it from that of affection.

The Four Types of Affect

- First, an affect is an affection that increases (*augetur*) the body's power of acting. Affect, in this case, expresses an increase in perfection. Joy, for example, inasmuch as it is 'man's passage from a lesser to a greater perfection',[77] fits into this first category and would appear to be the ultimate prototype of the primary affect that increases the *potentia agendi*.
- Second, affect is an affection that diminishes (*minuitur*) the body's power of acting. Affect, in this case, corresponds to a decrease in our perfection. Sadness, inasmuch as it is 'man's passage from a greater to a lesser perfection'[78] would appear to be the very illustration of this second category of affects, and thus serves as a counterweight to joy.

---

[77] *Ethics* III, DA 2; CWS I, 531.
[78] Ibid.

The first pair of opposites does not pose any major problems. It conveys the quantitative modifications of the power of acting and the variations in its degree of reality. Spinoza unambiguously suggests this in his general definition of the affects, although his comments concern the power of the mind:

> So when I said above that the Mind's power of Thinking is increased or diminished, I meant nothing but that the Mind has formed of its Body (or of some part of it) an idea which expresses more or less reality than it had affirmed of the Body.[79]

- Third, an affect is an affection that aids (*juvatur*) the power of acting. The verb *juvare*, which means to aid, to help or to assist, refers to the idea of an auxiliary cause favourable to the power of acting.
- Lastly, an affect is an affection that constrains or impedes (*coërcetur*) the power of acting. The verb *coërcere*, which means to enclose, to hold or to repress, suggests the idea of a constraint and involves the existence of a preventing cause that curbs the power of acting, keeping it within limits. *Coërcere* is also a term Spinoza uses to describe the activity of reason, inasmuch as it opposes the affects. *Ethics* V thus proposes to determine the power of reason, and to 'show, above all, how great its dominion over the affects is, and what kind of dominion it has for constraining and moderating (*coërcendum et moderandum*) them.'[80]

Although *coërcere* can take on a broad meaning, we must nevertheless reject both Curley's English translation of it as 'restrains' and Appuhn's translation of it as *réduire* ('to reduce'), because it implies a reduction in the power of acting, which is not systematically contained in this verb. The verb, of course, implies a

---

[79] *Ethics* III, General Definition of the Affects, Exp.; CWS I, 542–3.
[80] *Ethics* V, Praef. Spinoza had already used this expression in the Preface to Part IV in order to define bondage as 'man's lack of power to moderate and constrain the affects (*moderandis et coërcendis affectibus*)'. Translation modified.

limitation but it does not necessarily take the shape of a reduction or a lessening. Translating *coërcere* as 'contain' or 'constrain', as Elwes and Parkinson do, on the other hand, may be a better fit; *'empêcher'* ('to prevent'), as French commentator Pierre Macherey proposes, or *'ostacolare'* in Giancotti and Cristofolini's Italian translations, are better; 'to curb' or 'to check', which is Shirley's choice, also seem to be well suited to the concept of power.

The second pair of opposites raises more questions than the first, since it seems to serve as a counterweight to the first pair in a purely rhetorical and redundant manner, such that most commentators implicitly consider this specification as a simple repetition intended to amplify the first formulation and they make no mention of it. The question arises, however, of whether it is purely an effect of style or whether, on the contrary, there is a real difference between increasing and aiding on the one hand and diminishing and constraining on the other. Do aid and constraint also convey variations of perfection and are they reducible to forms of increasing and diminishing, or do they have an irreducible specificity?

To this end, we must first observe that Spinoza reiterates this double formulation throughout Part III,[81] such that it is unlikely that it can be reduced to a simple form of insistence. Second, it must be noted that when the author mentions only a single pair of opposites, he refers more often to the second, such that the affections that aid or constrain are not epiphenomena but instead take centre stage, to the point of obscuring those that increase or diminish the body's power of acting.[82] Lastly, it must also be noted

---

[81] Cf. *Ethics* III, 11–13, III, 19 Dem., III, 37 Dem., III, 57 Dem., III, General Definition of the Affects, IV, 8 Dem., I, 18 Dem., IV, 29 Dem. IV, 41 Dem., IV, 42 Dem., IV, 59 Dem.

[82] The occurrences of the verbs 'increase' and 'diminish', used either together or separately with regard to the affections, without being followed by the verbs 'aid' or 'constrain' are infrequent, and come up about ten times: *'Increase' and 'diminish' together*: *Ethics* III, 15, III, General Definition of the Affects, Exp., IV, 1 Schol., IV, 7 Dem. *'Increase' alone*: *Ethics* III, 43; IV, 46. *'Diminish' alone*: *Ethics* III, 48 Dem.

On the other hand, cases of 'aid' and, especially, 'constrain' that are not preceded by 'increase' or 'diminish' occur much more frequently. *'Aid' and*

that the affections aiding or constraining the power of acting also express the passage from a lesser to a greater perfection or, conversely, from a greater to a lesser one, since they respectively produce the affects of joy and sadness. This is what emerges in particular from the demonstration of Proposition 19 of *Ethics* III:

> Therefore, the images of things that posit the existence of a thing loved aid the Mind's striving to imagine the thing loved, that is (by ll S), affect the Mind with Joy. On the other hand, those which exclude the existence of a thing loved constrain the same striving of the Mind, that is (by PllS), affect the Mind with Sadness.[83]

This statement is not an isolated or accidental formulation, since Spinoza defines joy as that which increases or aids the body's power of acting, and sadness as that which diminishes or constrains it in the demonstration of Proposition 41 of *Ethics* IV: 'Joy (by III, ll and ll S) is an affect by which the body's power of acting is increased or aided. Sadness, on the other hand, is an affect by which the body's power of acting is diminished or constrained.'[84] Generally, the affections that increase or aid the power of acting are equated with something good – in other words 'what we certainly know to be useful to us'[85] – and the affections that diminish or constrain with something evil.[86]

'constrain' together: *Ethics* IV, 29 Dem. 'Aid': *Ethics* III, 19 Dem., III, 20 Dem., III, 21 Dem., III, 34 Dem., III, 44 Dem., IV, 51 Alt. Dem., IV, 53 Dem., IV App. 7; IV App. 30.

'Constrain': *Ethics* III, 19 Dem., III, 23 Dem., III, 35 Dem., III, 38 Dem., III, 39 Schol., III, 47 Schol., III, 51 Schol.; III, 55 Dem., III, 55 Cor. Dem., III DA 41, III DA 42, IV, 7 Dem., IV, 15 and Dem., IV, 16 and Dem., IV, 17, IV, 29 and Dem., IV, 37 Schol. 2, IV, 43 Dem., IV, 47 Dem., IV, 53 Dem., IV, 60 Dem., IV, 62 Schol; IV, 59 Dem., V Praef., V, 7 Dem., V, 10 Schol., V, 42 and Dem.

[83] Translation modified.

[84] Translation modified. Cf. also *Ethics* III, 37, Dem.; CWS I, 515 'Sadness diminishes or constrains a man's power of acting.' Translation modified.

[85] Cf. *Ethics* IV, Def. 1; CWS I, 546.

[86] Cf. *Ethics* IV, 29; CWS I, 560: 'we call good or evil what is the cause of Joy or Sadness [. . .], that is [. . .]; what increases or diminishes, aids or constrains, our power of acting.' Translation modified.

This state of affairs has two consequences. First, supposing the affections that aid or constrain do not increase or diminish the power of acting, they must nevertheless have an impact on it, be useful or harmful to it, and vary its perfection in some way or another. For aid and constraint to be worthy of the name 'affect' and to differentiate themselves from states that remain simple affections, they must produce effects that modify the power of acting in a joyous or sad manner. They thus fall under the category of intermediate affections, between states that increase or diminish the power of acting, and those that are indifferent and neutral.

Second, although the affections that aid or constrain the power of acting cannot be reduced to those that increase or diminish it, they are not fundamentally dissimilar. This is because they boil down to joy and sadness, and express a path towards a greater or lesser perfection. Affects, consequently, are all by nature states of transition in the power of acting, so there is necessarily continuity between aid and increase, constraint and decrease. Although their effects are different, they are not divergent.

The question arises, however, as to whether affect always involves a variation of power – a transition – particularly when the activity is such that nothing can constrain it. Indeed, when we are the adequate cause of affects, we express a greater perfection thanks to the internal development of our power of acting. We strengthen our power of connecting the body's affections according to the order of the intellect, relating them to the idea of God, such that we would be affected by a love of God.[87] The threshold issue then arises. If active joy, as expressing the shift from a lesser to a greater affection, is undeniably an affect, what of beatitude, which, as perfection itself, no longer seems to allow transition? Presented as a virtue,[88] beatitude, of course, consists of 'a constant and eternal Love of God'[89] but is it necessarily an affect?

In opposition to Wetlesen's arguments[90], Michael Scrijvers

---

[87] Cf. *Ethics* V, 39 Dem.; CWS I, 614.

[88] *Ethics* V, 42; CWS I, 616.

[89] *Ethics* V, 36 Schol.

[90] Cf. *The Sage and the Way: Spinoza's Ethics of Freedom* (Assen, Van Gorcum, 1979), p. 103.

considers beatitude to be an affect, since it still involves a transition. In the case of active joy, the transition consists of adding adequate ideas, connected in actual existence to the development of inadequate ideas functioning as a trigger for the former. A similar transition must occur in the case of beatitude, because the act of acquiring this perfection does not succeed without difficulty.[91]

In order to settle the debate, we must observe that Spinoza does not strictly equate beatitude with the intellectual love of God but with love towards God, whether it is presented as constant and eternal, as in the Scholium to *Ethics* V, 36, or as a simple *amor erga Deum*, as in the demonstration of *Ethics* V, 41. This statement means that blessedness, in turn, takes the form of *amor erga Deum*, when it is related to the mind and the body actually existing, or the form of the intellectual love of God, when it is related to the mind alone. In the first case it is characterised by its constancy, in the second by its eternity. It is clearly because it is encompassed by the *amor erga Deum* and the *amor intellectualis Deum* that beatitude is described as a constant and eternal love of God. These two adjectives, which may seem redundant, do not refer to the same thing. One applies to the love of God related to both mind and body, and the other to the love of God related to the mind alone. The question of whether beatitude is an affect therefore has two sides and perhaps requires different approaches, depending on whether we are dealing with

[91] 'The Conatus and the Mutual Relationship Between Active and Passive Affects in Spinoza', in Y. Yovel (ed.), *Desire and Affect: Spinoza as Psychologist*, pp. 77–8: 'Nevertheless in the case of *beatitudo*, there is also – necessarily – a "transition"; otherwise it would lose all its affective significance, which it unquestionably has. This can be explained as follows. In the case of active joy, the transition consists in an addition of adequate ideas, which, in actual existence, is connected with the development of inadequate ideas that function as the occasion for provoking the former. A *similar* transition must occur in the case of *beatitudo*. Spinoza's qualification of *beatitudo* as the very possession of perfection (rather than a transition towards perfection) does not exclude, by definition, *all transition*, as Wetlesen wrongly believes. The notion of transition is still valid here because the act of entering in possession of this perfection, under the specific conditions of actuality, does not succeed – as Spinoza himself remarks – without a great deal of difficulty (*Ethics* V, 42s).'

amor erga Deum or with *amor intellectualis*. It is clear that love
of God is an affect. Spinoza openly states it in the Scholium to
Proposition 20 of *Ethics* V: 'So we can conclude that this Love
is the most constant of all the affects, and insofar as it is related
to the Body, cannot be destroyed, unless it is destroyed with the
Body itself.' Beatitude as love towards God allows transitions in
the power of acting, not only because it stops with death but also
because it is liable to increase proportionately with the body's
capabilities and with the greatness of the eternal part of the mind.
Thus, 'the more the Mind enjoys this divine Love, or beatitude,
the more it understands (by 32), that is (by 3 Cor.), the greater
the power it has over the affects, and (by 38) the less it is acted
on by evil affects'.[92] On the other hand, the intellectual love of
God, inasmuch as it is related to the mind alone, does not bring
the body's affections into play and does not seem susceptible to
variation, since it does not encounter any evil affects. Indeed,
'only while the Body endures is the Mind subject to affects which
are related to the passions'.[93] When Spinoza analyses intellectual
love, he never uses the word 'affect' to refer to it. However, the
intellectual love of God is equated with an action in *Ethics* V, 31,
such that it necessarily belongs to the category of affects of which
we are the adequate cause. It is defined as an action that does
not increase perfection, but is perfection itself. It thus expresses
the apex of the power of acting and of the dynamic nature of the
intellect that understands.

On the basis of these observations, it is now a question of analysing the status of these affections that aid or constrain in detail,
and to determine why Spinoza includes four types of modification
of the power of acting in his definition of the affects, instead of just
limiting himself to increase and decrease. To what could affections that are affects, although they do not increase nor diminish
the power of acting, refer?

A part of the answer appears in Proposition 15 of *Ethics* III,
which examines the case of when 'the Mind is affected by two
affects at once, one of which neither increases nor diminishes its

[92] *Ethics* V, 42 Dem.; CWS I, 616. Translation modified.
[93] *Ethics* V, 34; CWS I, 611.

power of acting, while the other either increases it or diminishes it'. When subsequently the mind is

> affected with the former affect as by its true cause, which (by hypothesis) through itself neither increases nor diminishes its power of thinking, it will immediately be affected with the latter also, which increases or diminishes its power of thinking, that is (by ll S), with Joy, or Sadness. And so the former thing will be the cause of Joy or Sadness – not through itself, but accidentally.

Under these circumstances, is it not possible to consider that a thing, which is accidentally the cause of joy or sadness, either by virtue of an association of ideas or a resemblance to an object that normally affects the mind with one or the other of these feelings, helps or constrains the power of acting? By definition, indeed, it neither increases nor diminishes it; nevertheless, it helps or curbs it by accidentally producing affects that increase or diminish this power.

This hypothesis is plausible, since it wholly corresponds to the case of affections that, by themselves, neither increase nor diminish the power of acting, all the while having an indirect impact on it. They therefore fit into the defined framework and belong to the category of that which aids or constrains. We must recognise, however, that Spinoza does not expressly use the verbs *juvare* or *coërcerce* to describe this scenario. That is why, in order to avoid arguable interpretations, we need only take into account occurrences of these verbs expressly applied to the power of acting, and use them as a basis to draw out their exact meaning and clearly identify the affects they concern.

The hypothesis sometimes put forward to explain the presence of the second pair of opposites when defining the affects consists in thinking that affections that aid the body's power of acting are those opposing the forces detrimental to it, and that those that constrain it are those opposing the forces favourable to it.[94] These

---

[94] Pascal Sévérac defends this hypothesis in *Le devenir actif chez Spinoza* (Paris: Honoré Champion, 2005).

affections neither increase nor diminish the power of acting; they only neutralise the detrimental or favourable powers by cancelling out their effects. Aid and constraint are conveyed by an increase or decrease, if the forces opposing the power of acting disappear. Meanwhile, aid would favour the power of acting, without necessarily increasing it, and constraint would block it, without necessarily diminishing it. Under these circumstances, aid would be only a positive form of constraint, reducible to the resistance with which the power of acting opposes hostile affections by curbing them. Therefore, the distinction between aiding and increasing, on the one hand, and constraining and diminishing, on the other, does not hinge on a difference of nature but on a difference of degree. Aiding and constraining would thus constitute the zero degree of increasing and diminishing, inasmuch as they initiate a qualitative change in the power that does not (or does not yet) express itself with a quantitative variation due to unfavourable circumstances.

As coherent as it may be, this hypothesis cannot explain all cases of aiding or blocking, although it accounts for some them. Indeed, although it is clear that Spinoza can think about constraint as a positive form of opposition to a force harmful to the power of acting – when he maintains, for example, that we need an equally great virtue of the mind to constrain blind daring as we do to constrain fear –[95] it is less obvious that he considers all aid in this manner, and that he reduces it systematically to striving to counteract an evil. In Chapter 7 of the Appendix to *Ethics* IV, he presents aid, on the contrary, as a positive force based on the agreement of natures, which expresses itself independently of the existence of obstacles: 'If he lives among such individuals as agree with his nature, his power of acting will thereby be aided (*juvabitur*) and encouraged.' Under these circumstances it would be difficult to accept that Spinoza conceives of aid as a simple force of opposition, since it expresses an actual agreement of powers that cannot be reduced to resistance. That is why it is necessary to define aid and constraint more precisely, in order to then be able to measure their impact on the power of acting.

[95] *Ethics* IV, 69 Dem.; CWS I, 585.

Aiding and Increasing

It emerges from Chapter 7 of the Appendix to *Ethics* IV that aid is based on a relationship of agreement (*convenientia*) between things, and is evidence of harmony in their natures. It therefore presupposes the presence of common characteristics among individuals. It is true that this observation is valid for all the affects to a certain extent. Their condition of possibility lies in the existence of a minimum of common properties among the powers of acting of things; without it, they would not be able to affect one another. Spinoza clearly emphasises this in Proposition 29 of *Ethics* IV: 'Any singular thing whose nature is entirely different from ours can neither aid nor constrain our power of acting.'[96] But while that which constrains opposes our power of acting and has very little in common with it, that which aids, on the contrary, favours it all the more since it shares a greater number of properties with it. That is why aid reaches its apex when it fundamentally expresses an agreement of natures. *Convenientia* should not be confused with a simple collection of shared properties, however. It is more than having properties in common: it expresses a shared nature. By the same token, affections that aid the power of acting must be sought in rational human individuals. Indeed, Spinoza maintains in Chapter 9 of the Appendix to *Ethics* IV that 'nothing can agree more with the nature of any thing than other individuals of the same species. And so (by VII) nothing is more useful to man in preserving his being and enjoying a rational life than a man who is guided by reason.' Maximum aid, consequently, is given by the active affects of desire and joy, and generally includes affections that are useful to our power.

This conclusion, however, is also valid, and all the more so for affections that increase the power of acting. Under these circumstances, how is aiding different from increasing? In order to understand the distinction, we must examine the conditions for increasing a thing, as they emerge from Proposition 43 of *Ethics* III, where Spinoza maintains that 'Hate is increased by being returned, but can be destroyed by Love.' In the demonstration he

---

[96] Translation modified.

justifies this mechanism of increase – which can be applied to love as well as to other affects – by the appearance of a new hate, while the other still exists. The quantity of initial hate towards the object of scorn is combined with a sadness linked to the fact that this thing hates us in return. This sadness is accompanied, by definition, with a hate for the cause bringing it about, a second hate that magnifies the first hostile affect. From there, it is possible to deduce that an affection increases the power of acting when it is added to a previous state of joy identical to it. In this case, the shift from a lesser to a greater perfection is conveyed by a quantitative increase in joy.

An affection aids the power of acting when it brings about a joy that does not become superimposed on a state of the same nature, because it is either contrary or different to it. In the first case, the shift from a lesser to a greater perfection is not expressed by an increase. Rather, it conveys an abrupt stop in the initial state of reduction and stagnation in the power of acting. The affection triggers a change of perspective, a reorientation of the *conatus* towards joy. It does not increase the power of acting; it favours it instead by counteracting the sad affects. Aid does not take the form of an accumulation of power, but of a drop in powerlessness. In the second case, joy produced by aid does not add to that of the power of acting and does not quantitatively increase its perfection. Thus, we observe that an agreement of natures among individuals makes them joyous and represents an aid, but does not lead to an intrinsic increase in the power of acting specific to each person, since the power of acting remains the same and is not extended by this simple observation. Similitude gives it more latitude but does not increase its amplitude. However, given that the power of acting of a thing refers to 'the striving by which it (either alone or with others) does anything, or strives to do anything',[97] it is clear that the agreement of natures is favourable to uniting forces and cooperation among individuals so that they can together produce the effects that a single individual would not have been able to accomplish. Of course, extrinsically, it would not be false to say, in light of the effects, that each person's power of acting is greatest

---

[97] Cf. *Ethics* III, 7 Dem.; CWS I, 499.

when people cooperate. But there is not necessarily an intrinsic increase in the perfection of each person here, since his power is simply strengthened, assisted by auxiliary causes. Consequently, aid in Spinoza is not reducible to a simple affection that opposes forces contrary to the *conatus*. It expresses the positive impact on the power of acting of external causes that agree with it in nature.

Diminishing and Constraining

Whether it takes on the power of acting, passive affects,[98] or a desire arising from the knowledge of good and evil,[99] the affection that constrains always expresses, in contrast, a relationship of opposition, despite the necessary minimal commonality of natures, and involves the existence of not only an opposing force but a superior one. This is what Proposition 7 of *Ethics* IV demonstrates: 'An affect cannot be constrained (*coërcei*) or taken away except by an affect opposite to, and stronger than, the affect to be constrained.'[100] Constraint therefore requires a force that prevails over the current state of the power of acting,[101] modifying it unfavourably. This condition also applies to all affections that diminish the power of acting. That which constrains is distinguished, however, from that which diminishes, since it holds back but does not suppress the power it opposes. It blocks the production of all its affects, suspending them but without necessarily destroying them. Thus, for example, the sadness with which we contemplate a thing we hate is a 'determination [which] is, indeed, constrained

---

[98] It is in this sense that the verb 'constrain' is used, for example, in *Ethics* V, 42 Dem.; CWS I, 616: 'no one enjoys blessedness because he has constrained the affects. Instead, the power to constrain lusts arises from blessedness itself, QED.' Translation modified.

[99] Cf. *Ethics* IV, 62 Schol.; CWS I, 582: 'the Desire which arises from a knowledge of good and evil, insofar as this looks to the future, can be rather easily constrained by a Desire for the pleasures of the moment.' Translation modified.

[100] Translation modified.

[101] This dominance of the force that constrains is also highlighted in *Ethics* IV, 60, where Spinoza considers the case of when 'part A is constrained so that the others prevail'. Translation modified.

(*coërcetur*) by the memory of those things that exclude its existence; but it is not taken away.'[102]

Diminishing, on the other hand, goes hand in hand with complete or partial removal. This is what emerges from Proposition 48 of *Ethics* III, where Spinoza demonstrates that love and hate for Peter, for example, are destroyed if the joy and sadness they involve are attached to the idea of another cause, and diminished if we imagine that Peter was not their sole cause. The intensity of the affect towards Peter is proportional to the part we imagine he plays in their formation. It is therefore a function of the cause we have attributed wholly or partially to Peter. 'If this is taken away – either wholly or in part – the affect toward Peter is also diminished, either wholly or in part.' The lessening of power therefore varies between two limits: an upper limit, when it is total and equivalent to elimination, and a lower limit, when the decline has barely begun. It takes the form of accommodation, of an adaptation to the power opposing it, to the point of becoming less and less contrary to it. The suppression of an affect presupposes its reduction to the contrary affect, such that they end up adapting to each other.[103]

An affection that constrains a state of the power of acting does not destroy it. Rather, it counterbalances its effects by either suspending or tempering them. In the first case the constraint leads to a balance of contrary powers and may generate a vacillation of mind that paralyses action. This is what results, for example, from consternation. 'If the desire to avoid a future evil is constrained by Timidity regarding another evil, so that he does not know what he would rather do, then the Fear is called Consternation, particularly if each evil he fears is of the greatest.'[104] In the second case,

---

[102] *Ethics* III, 47 Schol.; CWS I, 520. Translation modified.

[103] This is what is highlighted in particular in *Ethics* V, 7 Dem.; CWS I, 600, which deals with the power of an affect arising from reason: 'such an affect will always remain the same, and hence (by AI), the affects which are contrary to it and are not encouraged by their external causes will have to accommodate themselves to it more and more, until they are no longer contrary to it. To that extent, an affect arising from reason is more powerful.'

[104] *Ethics* III, 39 Schol.; CWS I, 516–17. Translation modified.

the constraining affection has a moderating effect. Thus, pain can be good insofar as it constrains pleasure (*titillatio*) and corrects its excesses.[105] It does not suppress the species of joy linked to pleasure, but moderates it by drawing attention to the fact that a part of the body is affected to the detriment of the others, consequently encouraging moderation. This explains the association of *coërcere* and *moderare* to describe the power of reason in the face of affects.[106]

At the end of this clarification of the nature of aid and constraint, it must be noted that the passage from a lesser to a greater perfection, or of a greater to a lesser one, does not systematically translate into a quantitative increase or decrease in the power of acting. Indeed, although aid leads to an improvement in the effectiveness specific to each individual, thanks to joining forces, it does not necessarily take the form of an increase. This observation makes it possible to clarify the meaning of the concept of passage (*transitio*) in Spinoza, and to cast a reflective light on the nature of joy and sadness, which are too hastily equated to increases or decreases in power. The passage from one degree of perfection to another is measured not only in terms of quantity but of quality as well. We still need to determine the exact nature of this transition carried out by the affections that aid or constrain within the power of acting, and to define precisely the affects belonging to this category.

An examination of the texts where the terms in question[107] appear reveals that, generally, that which aids or constrains is connected to the consequences of the variations in the powers of things and others on my own power, and involves relationships to the thing we love and to the thing we hate, as well as, more generally, relationships to other people similar to ourselves. These affections are subsequent to the real or imaginary increase or decrease in the power of things we love, hate or that are similar, and express their indirect consequences on us. This explains why

---

[105] Cf. *Ethics* IV, 43 Dem.; *CWS* I, 570.

[106] Cf. *Ethics* V, Praef.

[107] See above for the inventory of occurrences of the verbs 'aid' and 'constrain'.

aid and constraint do not increase or diminish our power of acting, since they are not connected to it and do not fundamentally call it into question. Rather, they concern the power of acting by others, while having collateral effects for us. On the basis of the inventory of the occurrences of the verbs, it is indeed possible to distinguish five main types of affection that aid or constrain.

1. What aids is whatever opposes the destruction of the thing we love or the preservation of the thing we hate.

Thus 'the images of things that posit the existence of a thing loved aid (*juvant*) the Mind's striving to imagine the thing loved, that is (by 11 Schol.), affect the Mind with Joy'.[108] Conversely, 'the image of a thing which excludes the existence of what the Mind hates aids (*juvat*) this striving of the Mind, that is (by 11 Schol.), it affects the Mind with Joy'.[109] This kind of affection refers to a type of joy arising either from the joy of the thing we love or from the sadness of the thing we hate. The image of the thing we love in jubilation does not increase my power of acting, since it involves the joy of another. It aids my striving, however, since it affirms the existence of the thing I love more strongly, seeing that it passes to a greater perfection and fills me with joy in return.[110] Similarly, the image of the sadness of the thing I hate aids my striving, since it tends to weaken the existence of what I abhor without necessarily increasing my reality. That is why 'he who imagines what he hates to be affected with sadness will rejoice'.[111] Symmetrically, that which constrains the power of acting is that which opposes the preservation the thing we love or the destruction of the thing we hate. Although 'the imagination is aided (*juvatur*) by what posits the existence of a thing', it is, on the other hand, 'constrained (*coërcetur*) by what excludes the existence of a thing'.[112] Thus the image of the sadness of the thing I love constrains my power of

---

108 *Ethics* III, 19; CWS I, 505.
109 *Ethics* III, 20; CWS I, 506.
110 *Ethics* III, 21 Dem.; CWS I, 506: 'the image in the lover of the loved thing's Joy aids his Mind's striving, that is (by 11 Schol.), affects the lover with Joy'.
111 *Ethics* III, 23; CWS I, 507.
112 *Ethics* III, 19 Dem.; CWS I, 505–6. Translation modified.

acting, such that I feel a form of pity. Although Spinoza does not name the affect of joy that arises from another's good fortune,[113] the affect of sadness linked to another's misfortune is none other than pity (*commiseratio*).[114] Commiseration is therefore among the affections that curb the power of acting – without diminishing it, however, since it does not attest to our own unhappiness but to that of another.

Similarly, the image of the joy of the thing we hate constrains us. 'If someone imagines him whom he hates to be affected with Joy, this imagination [. . .] will constrain (*coërcibit*) his striving.'[115] This sentiment corresponds to a species of envy (*invidia*), which 'is nothing but Hate, insofar as it is considered so to dispose a man that he is glad at another's ill fortune and saddened by his good fortune'.[116] Envy is explicitly presented as an affect that constrains the power of acting in the demonstration of the second corollary of Proposition 55 of *Ethics* III. 'Envy is Hatred itself [. . .], a Sadness, that is [. . .], an affection by which a man's power of acting, or striving, is constrained (*coërcetur*).'[117] Equating this feeling to an affection contrary to the *conatus* is somewhat problematic, however, since it would seem that envy, to the extent that it encourages us to rejoice at another's ill fortune, aids our striving when we hate the victim. In reality, envy does not aid, because the joy we feel when seeing the ills of a hated being is not static; it always involves a wavering of mind and continues to be characterised by sadness, seeing that the other is like us.[118] Now, according to Proposition 27 of *Ethics* III, the image of the sadness affecting a thing like us makes us sad. This makes it possible to understand in turn that pity can extend to all similar beings and not only to the thing we love, and that the sight of the misfortune of another affects us with sadness and constrains our striving.

---

[113] Cf. *Ethics* III, 22 Schol.; CWS I, 507: 'By what name we should call the Joy which arises from another's good I do not know.'

[114] Ibid.

[115] *Ethics* III, 23 Dem.; CWS I, 507. Translation modified.

[116] *Ethics* III, 24 Schol.; CWS I, 507.

[117] Translation modified.

[118] This is what emerges from *Ethics* III, 33.

2. The image of the joy affecting the thing we love on our account aids our striving.

'The greater the Joy with which we imagine a thing we love to be affected on our account, the more this striving is aided, that is (by 11 and BS), the greater the Joy with which we are affected.'[119] This joy with which we contemplate is none other than a particular species of the love of esteem arising from when a person believes himself to be esteemed by a beloved being.[120] This love of esteem is an affect that aids our power of acting, since it expresses the internal impact of joy caused by us, which is felt by the beloved thing and echoes its passage toward a greater perfection.

Although the joy of the beloved thing provoked by our efforts aids our power, the joy aroused by the efforts of another, on the other hand, constrains it. Indeed, he who loves tries to imagine the thing he loves to be bound to him as closely as possible. 'But this striving, or appetite, is supposed to be constrained by the image of the thing he loves, accompanied by the image of him with whom the thing he loves is united.'[121] He will therefore be affected by sadness, then hate, towards the thing he loves and its lover, towards whom he will also feel envy. He will then feel jealousy, this affect of hate toward the beloved thing combined with envy.[122] Jealousy does not diminish the power of acting, because the union of the thing I love with another does not take away from my perfection. Instead, jealousy constrains it by its sad nature.

3. The appearance of a reversal of feelings constrains or aids the power of acting.

This depends on whether feelings change from friendly to hostile or vice versa, before diminishing or increasing. Thus, nascent hate towards a beloved thing constrains the power of acting, all the more so as the love preceding it was great.[123] Indeed, joyous striving to remain beside the beloved sees itself counteracted by

---

[119] *Ethics* III, 34 Dem.; CWS I, 513–14.
[120] *Ethics* III, 30 Schol; CWS I, 511–12.
[121] *Ethics* III, 35 Dem.; CWS I, 514. Translation modified.
[122] *Ethics* III, 35 Dem. and Schol.; CWS I, 514.
[123] *Ethics* III, 38; CWS I, 515.

sadness linked to hate. Conversely, an affect of hate vanquished by budding love represents an aid all the more considerable since the hate preceding it was great.[124] In this case, to the joy of love 'there is also added a Joy arising from this – the striving to remove the Sadness hate involves [. . .] is wholly aided'.[125] This joy is accompanied by 'the idea of the one he hated'.[126] The case of the reversal of feelings is of particular interest, because it presents the beginnings of the change in the form of aid and constraint, then its development in the form of an increase or decrease in the power of acting inversely proportional to the greatness of the affect of hate or love felt before. It thus corroborates the hypothesis of continuity between the four forms of affection, and shows aid and constraint as the beginning of an increase or decrease.

4. Someone who benefits another supports our striving to do the same.

The affect of favour, as love for someone who benefits another,[127] fits into the category of affects that aid the power of acting. It can be a passion as well as an action arising from reason. Thus the reasonable person, 'because he sees someone benefiting another, his own striving to do good is aided, that is (by III, 11 Schol.), he will rejoice'.[128] The aid is indirect, since it involves affective mimicry, and results from the love felt for someone who has not benefited me, but a third party. Favour is therefore the impact of increasing the power of another on my power.

Curiously, indignation, which is the opposite of favour, since it is defined as 'a Hate towards someone who has done evil to another',[129] is not explicitly presented as an affect that constrains the power of acting. This asymmetry may stem from the particular nature of this passion that can help as well as harm the power by inciting reprisals against the author of the heinous acts. It is

[124] Cf. *Ethics* III, 44; CWS I, 519.
[125] Ibid.
[126] Ibid.
[127] *Ethics* III, DA 19; CWS I, 535.
[128] *Ethics* IV, 51 Alt. Dem.; CWS I, 574.
[129] *Ethics* III, DA 20; CWS I, 535.

thus the driver of political revolt, and may help put an end to injustice.[130] Saying, on that basis, that it is among the affects that aid the power of acting is a step that Spinoza does not take. Indignation is indeed an ambiguous affect, since it can lead to taking the law into your own hands and to favouring power, but, in so doing, it helps establish a lawless state where everyone tries to seize power, and consequently weakens their own force of existing by harming the security of the state. This is what Spinoza highlights in Chapter 24 of the Appendix to *Ethics* IV: 'Though Indignation seems to present an appearance of fairness, nevertheless, when everyone is allowed to pass judgement on another's deeds, and to vindicate either his own or another's right, we live without a law.'[131]

5. Affections arising from adequate or inadequate conceptions of human powerlessness aid or constrain the power of acting.

If a man, in considering himself, perceives some lack of power of his, this is not because he understands himself but because his power of acting is constrained (as we have shown in III, 55). But if we suppose that the man conceives his lack of power because he understands something more powerful than himself, by the knowledge of which he determines his power of acting, then we conceive nothing but that the man understands himself distinctly or (by III, 26) that his power of acting is aided.[132]

Here, that which aids and that which constrains correspond to two different ways, one adequate and the other inadequate, of understanding the same thing. It is therefore not human powerlessness that constrains power but the way in which it is conceived. Aid and constraint do not result from the nature of the thing, but from the cognitive relationship we have with them. In the first case, the affect felt is humility, which arises when a person contemplates his own powerlessness. Humility is a sad passion that constrains the

---

[130] Cf. *TP* IV, 4 and IV, 6; *CWS* II, 526 and 528.
[131] Translation modified.
[132] *Ethics* IV, 53 Dem.; *CWS* I, 575–6. Translation modified.

power of acting. This is what emerges from the demonstration of Proposition 55 of *Ethics* III:

> So when we say that the Mind, in considering itself, imagines its lack of power, we are saying nothing but that the Mind's striving to imagine something which posits its power of acting is constrained, or (by ll Schol.) that it is saddened.[133]

Indeed, there is no powerlessness in itself, since each thing is as perfect as it can be. On the other hand, if a person does not consider this lack of power under the influence of a sad humility but, rather, from an understanding of something more powerful than himself, his power of acting will be aided. The affect that aids here does not have a name, and could correspond to a virtuous humility, in contrast with humility as a vice. However, this concept, which is present in Descartes, does not appear in Spinoza and is inappropriate, since in reality it is a question of understanding our own powerlessness as a particular power. Indeed, we understand our lack of power not as a consequence of a lack or an intrinsic imperfection, but as a power determined by God's infinite power. This unnamed affect is an aid, because we understand ourselves as a part of Nature and we feel joy, but it does not increase our power of acting, which remains determined. It appears as a form of satisfaction (*acquiescientia*), since it implies that we are conscious of ourselves, of things, and of God, and that we understand that our power is limited and infinitely surpassed by that of external causes. This is what Spinoza suggests in Chapter 23 of the Appendix to *Ethics* IV: 'If we understand this clearly and distinctly, that part of us which is defined by understanding, that is, the better part of us, will be entirely satisfied with this, and will strive to persevere in that satisfaction.'

Ultimately, whether it is joy arising from the happiness of the beloved thing or the sadness of a thing we hate, pity or envy, love of esteem or jealousy, the nascent reversal of feelings or favour, affections that aid or constrain the power of acting are not only those that oppose favourable or unfavourable forces. Rather, they

[133] Translation modified.

more generally concern the effects of the power of another on our own, and its indirect consequences. They mostly involve affective imitation and fall under an ethics of similitude. This imitation takes either the form of echoing the good or ill fortune of another, or the opposite stance from the affects of the thing we hate. But, whether it is identical or reversed, the image that our power of acting reflects of another's is always a matter of affective mimicry.

The fifth type of affect, however, would seem to partially contradict these conclusions. Satisfaction belongs, if need be, to the framework of mimetic affects linked to the perception of likeness, agreements or disagreements, seeing that it stems from the confrontation of the body's power of acting with Nature's, and results from the comprehension of something more powerful. Humility, on the other hand, is seen as an exception, since it involves a relationship with oneself and one's own lack of power. In reality, the image of powerlessness arises from an idea that excludes our body's existence. Yet, this idea, strictly speaking, is not in us, because the mind affirms the body's actual existence and does not exclude it. This idea, therefore, does not refer to God inasmuch as he constitutes the nature of our mind, but to God inasmuch as he constitutes the nature of other things. It brings into play the common order of Nature, and the existence of external causes. It expresses their impact on our power in the inadequate form of humility. Consequently, this affect also expresses the effects of an imaginative perception of the power of the external world. It makes it possible to extend the scope of the affects of aid or constraint, not only to the things we love and hate and to the other as someone like us, but to anything that expresses an agreement or disagreement with our power. Thus, that which aids and constrains falls under an ethics of similitude and involves relationships among individuals, whether these individuals are in the form of physical, human or political bodies. In short, affections that aid or constrain our power of acting are the mirror images of those affecting individuals of *natura naturata*, and more particularly other people, by virtue of a shared resemblance. This explains why they occur more frequently, since people live with other people and are constantly affected by them.

The Mental Aspect of Affect and the Meaning of the Adverb Simul

Having analysed affect in its corporeal dimension and shed light on its various forms, we must now account for its mental aspect, because it not only covers affections that increase or diminish, aid or constrain the power of acting, but also the ideas of these affections. Although commentators agree in recognising that affect involves a *'face physique'* as well as a *'face mentale'*,[134] they diverge as to the constitution of the coin. Can one side, given that it has a physical or mental flipside, form an affect on its own, or do we have to take both sides into account? Can an affect still be on the money if we only consider one side? Beyond the metaphor, the question is what the exact meaning of the adverb *simul* is in Definition 3. Whether it is translated by the adverb 'at the same time', 'together' or 'also', the problem remains the same. The expression *'et simul'* can have a conjunctive or distributive meaning, to use Jean-Marie Beyssade's[135] formulation, such that the definition can be interpreted in two ways. On the one hand, it may mean that, in order to form, affect necessarily always combines an affection and an idea of this affection, and simultaneously expresses a physical and

---

[134] The expression [TN: meaning a physical and a mental side, as of a coin] is Pierre Macherey's, in his *Introduction à l'Ethique de Spinoza*, Part III, p. 27.

[135] 'What does the "at the same time" (*et simul*), which adds to element (a) another element (b), mean? It may have two different functions. On the one hand, it may be conjunctive: the affect would then require the conjunction of a physiological aspect (the "affections of the body", in (a), which are not yet affects) and at the same time a mental or conscious aspect (the "ideas of those affections" in (b), which must be added in order to transform the affections of the body into a genuine affect). On the other hand, it may be distributive: it may apply the name of affect simultaneously to certain corporeal affections (those that increase or diminish the body's power to act, something that does not require the mind's intervention at all) and, in parallel and at the same time, to the ideas of these corporeal affections, ideas that according to Spinoza's parallelism, always accompany by nature (*simul esse natura*) their physiological counterparts.' '*Nostri Corporis Affectus*: Can an affect in Spinoza Be "of the Body"?' in Y. Yovel (ed.), *Desire and Affect: Spinoza as Psychologist*, p. 115.

a mental reality. In this case, affect would concern a human being as a body *and* a mind. There could not be, strictly speaking, affects of the body, but all bodily affects must necessarily be conscious in order to be transformed into affects. On the other hand, it may mean that by affect Spinoza either means an affection of the body that increases or diminishes, aids or constrains this body's power of acting, or an idea of this affection, or both. In this case, affect would concern a human being not only as a mind *and* a body, but also as a mind *or* a body. There would therefore be affects of the mind or affects of the body that, of course, would have their physical or mental correlate by virtue of the unity of the human being and its two modal expressions in the attribute of extension and in the attribute of thought. However, they would be formed as such without the intervention of this correlate. The question, then, is what exactly is covered by the term 'affect'?

Affect and Consciousness

If, in order to be formed, affects involve a state of mind as well as a bodily state, it is clear that affective life is characterised above all by the consciousness of emotions. This is what is suggested by the corollary to Proposition 4 in *Ethics* V, which states that 'an affect is an idea of the affection of the Body'. Of course, this catchphrase taken literally does not identify affect with awareness but with an idea of a corporeal affection, whether it is adequate or inadequate. However, this shift from knowledge to consciousness is allowable, since Spinoza expressly equates the two in the demonstration of Proposition 9 of *Ethics* III. To set up the argument that the mind is conscious of its striving in order to persevere in its being, he highlights that the latter is *conscious of itself* through ideas of the body's affections. To justify his assertion, he refers to Proposition 23 of Part II, where he established that the mind *knows itself* though perceptions of bodily affections. Consciousness and knowledge are therefore synonymous terms.

But can we allow ourselves, on the basis of the corollary of Proposition 4 in *Ethics* IV, to conclude that any affect, by definition, presupposes consciousness and could not be formed without it? This is the position of Robert Misrahi, for whom affect concerns the mind as it is conscious of the body, while affection only relates to the body.[136] In his view, *simul* therefore necessarily has a conjunctive meaning, such that bodily affection is an essential but never sufficient condition for the creation of an affect. Consciousness is required for simple affection to give rise to an affect.

Besides the fact that the term 'affection' does not refer only to the body,[137] since it is synonymous with 'mode' and expresses all the ways of being of substance and of its attributes, Robert Misrahi's argument comes up against two major objections. First, although affect is always perceived by the mind, if only confusedly, this consciousness is not decisive in Spinoza. Of course, the primitive affect of desire, which is presented at the same time as constituting human essence, is defined as a conscious appetite[138] and could not be conceived without the reflexivity of the idea of striving to persevere in being. Nevertheless, we must not place too much importance on the phenomenon of consciousness, because it does not change the nature of the *conatus*. Spinoza emphasises this point in Definition 1 of the Affects: 'I really recognise no difference between human appetite and Desire. For whether a man is conscious of his appetite or not, the appetite still remains one and the same.' Although by nature related to the body as well as the mind,[139] appetite is therefore not essentially defined by consciousness, so we must not treat the phenomenon as a concrete reality. If appetite remains the same thing regardless of the case, this implies that consciousness does not transform its nature. If, in truth, desire

---

[136] Cf. note p. 401 of his translation of the Ethics: 'L'*affectus* est une conscience : l'esprit est toujours conscient du *conatus* et des idées claires ou confuses, qui constituent cet esprit (*Ethics* III, 9), et l'affect est l'idée (claire ou confuse d'une modification du corps.' [The *affectus* is awareness: the mind is always conscious of the *conatus* and of the clear or confused ideas that constitute this mind (*Ethics* III, 9), and affect is an idea (that is clear or confused) of a modification of the body.]

[137] Jean-Marie Beyssade points out that this term is also used with respect to the mind in *Ethics* III, 52 Schol. (*haec mentis affectio, sive res singularis imaginatio*), 'Nostri Corporis Affectus: Can an Affect in Spinoza be "of the Body"?' in Y. Yovel (ed.), *Desire and Affect: Spinoza as Psychologist*, p. 123.

[138] *Ethics* III, 9 Schol.; CWS I, 500.

[139] Ibid.

is an affect indistinguishable from appetite, this means that consciousness is not a fundamental expression of its essence, since it may disappear without its nature being changed. Thus this desiring nature that forms the substrate of all affects is not defined first and foremost by consciousness, since it is a second, or even a secondary, determination.

Does this mean that there could be desires, and therefore affects, that are unconscious? Spinoza does not go that far. He considers the hypothesis that a person is not conscious as an eventuality, without necessarily positively asserting that there actually are unconscious appetites. Complete unconsciousness would seem to be impossible, as the demonstration of Proposition 9 of *Ethics* III points out: 'Since the Mind (by II, 23) is necessarily conscious of itself through ideas of the Body's affections, the Mind (by 7) is conscious of its striving.' The argument put forward in Definition 1 aims to show not only that appetites or desires are unconscious but that this unconsciousness does not modify the nature of the thing. Spinoza recognises that he 'could have said that Desire is man's very essence, insofar as it is conceived to be determined to do something',[140] and therefore define it in the same way as appetite.[141] But, by his own admission, he did not wish to explain desire by appetite, because this definition would have resembled a tautology and would not have covered the cause of consciousness. That is why, 'in order to involve the cause of this consciousness, it was necessary [. . .] to add: *insofar as it is conceived, from some given affection of it, to be determined, etc.*' Consciousness is a property that must be explained. It accompanies appetite, but does this mean that they always go hand in hand? If desire is appetite with consciousness of the appetite (*appetitus cum ejusdem conscientia*),[142] we must question the value of this '*cum*', of this accompaniment of appetite by consciousness. When Spinoza maintains that he 'could have said that Desire is man's very essence, insofar as it is conceived to be determined to do something', in order to show that there was no difference in nature between desire and appe-

[140] *Ethics* III, DA 1 Exp.; CWS I, 531.
[141] Cf. *Ethics* III, 9 Schol.; CWS I, 500.
[142] Ibid.

tite, he justifies the necessity of a complement by saying 'from this definition [. . .] it would not follow that the Mind could be conscious of its Desire, or appetite (*non sequeretur, quod mens possit suae cupiditatis, sive appetitus esse conscia*)'. It should be noted that Spinoza writes: 'it would not follow that the Mind *could be conscious*', and not 'it would not follow that the Mind *is conscious*'. Consciousness is therefore a capability but this does not mean that it is fully realised in all the affects, to the point of constituting them as affects. Thus, for Spinoza, the ignorant man 'lives as if he knew neither (*quasi inscius*) himself, nor God, nor things',[143] and yet he is prey to affects, particularly sadness but also joy, because he is acted upon. Of course, he is 'unable ever to possess true peace of mind, [. . .] and as soon as he ceases to be acted on, he ceases to be'.[144] Nevertheless, although he is virtually unaware, he is buffeted by a multitude of passive affects. It is therefore going too far to define affects by consciousness, because this property does not accompany all of them in the same way, and expresses itself with difficulty through the emotions of the ignorant man, to the point where they can be considered to be quasi unconscious. Of course, the ignorant man's virtual unawareness will always be a form of minimal consciousness, such that there are no completely unconscious affects. It is not appropriate, however, to conceive of consciousness as a constituent reality of affect, seeing that it is not an absolute given or a native phenomenon. Consciousness is, in fact, less constituent than constituted, since it emerges through ideas of the body's affections. Spinoza recalls in Proposition 30 of *Ethics* III that 'man [. . .] is conscious of himself through the affections by which he is determined to act'. These affections that determine him to act are primary, and without them no consciousness is possible. If consciousness necessarily accompanies active affects, it is more uncertain in passive affects, since a human being perceives his appetite but does not know what causes him to act. From a mental point of view, affect therefore includes more or less consciousness, depending on whether its nature is more or less active. Affect expresses degrees of consciousness that range

---

[143] *Ethics* V, 42 Schol.; CWS I, 616–17.
[144] Ibid.

from the ignorant man's virtual unawareness to the clear and distinct consciousness of the wise man. It is not, however, defined with respect to this consciousness, since desire in the broad sense covers all of humanity's strivings, appetites and volitions. Spinoza hardly sees any harm, indeed, in encompassing 'all the strivings of human nature that we signify by the name of appetite, will, desire or impulse'[145] under the term 'desire'. Now, although volition is always conscious, since it is a mode of thought – although appetite could be, since it is related to the mind and body – impulse (*impetus*) alone would not appear to include consciousness, since it is related to the body above all. Does this mean that it is only explained by the relationship to the attribute of extension and excludes all reference to thought? There is no evidence to say so with complete certainty. On the other hand, if the term 'desire' in the broad sense covers all of humanity's strivings[146] without exception, it also includes the body's determinations, which by definition do not encompass consciousness. Although the body's determinations go together with appetite and with the mind's decrees, and are one with them, they are only explained with reference to extension and the laws of movement and rest.[147] This observation suggests that there could be bodily affects, and invites us to meditate upon this eventuality.

It is then possible to formulate a second objection to Robert Misrahi's argument. Not only is affect not essentially defined by consciousness, but it is also not necessarily a mental phenomenon. This argument is put forward by Jean-Marie Beyssade, who draws attention to the fact that there are not only affections but also affects of the body,[148] of which the mind, of course, has an idea, but which would be conceived of as modes of extension, like movement and rest. Indeed, Spinoza explicitly refers to such affects for

---

[145] *Ethics* III, DA 1 Exp.; CWS I, 531.

[146] Spinoza understands it in this sense at the end of the DA 1 Exp.: 'Here, therefore, by the word Desire I understand any of a man's strivings, impulses, appetites, and volitions.'

[147] Cf. *Ethics* III, 2 Schol.; CWS I, 494–7.

[148] Cf. his article '*Nostri Corporis Affectus*: Can an Affect in Spinoza Be "of the Body"?' in Y. Yovel (ed.), *Desire and Affect: Spinoza as Psychologist*, pp. 113–28.

the first time in Proposition 17 of *Ethics* II.[149] Admittedly, the presence of the expression '*corpus afficiatur affectu*' in Part II does not allow us to draw general conclusions, since the concept of affect has not yet been defined in its strict sense. Nevertheless, this is not due to a slip-up or a misprint, since Spinoza reiterates this wording in the demonstration of Proposition 14 of *Ethics* III: 'The imaginations of the Mind indicate the affects of our Body (*nostri corporis affectus*) more than the nature of external bodies.' He also alludes to 'the constitution of the body, or affect (*constitutio seu affectus*)' in the demonstration of Proposition 18 of *Ethics* III; then in Scholium 1 to the fact that 'the Body is not affected by any affect (*corpus nullo affectu afficitur*) that excludes the thing's existence.'

These occurrences of the concept of *affectus* applied to the body, as inventoried by Jean-Marie Beyssade, must be added to the fact that Spinoza maintains in Proposition 2 of *Ethics* III that 'the order of actions and passions of our Body is, by nature, at one (*simul*) with the order of actions and passions of the Mind'. Yet whether they are related to the mind or body, actions and passions are affects by definition. In *Ethics* V, finally, Spinoza maintains that 'we regard a thing as absent, not because of the affect by which we imagine it, but because the Body is affected by another affect which excludes the thing's existence'.[150]

There can therefore be no doubt: there really are bodily affects.[151] This observation leads to two major consequences. First, we must not interpret the corollary of Proposition 4 of *Ethics* V, according to which 'an affect is an idea of an affection of the Body', as the statement of a complete general definition of affect, excluding the possibility of bodily affects, but rather a particular statement regarding its mental aspect. It is therefore incorrect to use this corollary as the basis for claiming that affect is defined above all by consciousness.

---

[149] 'If the human Body is affected with a mode that involves the nature of an external body, the human Mind will regard the same external body as actually existing, or as present to it, until the *Body is affected by an affect* (*corpus afficiatur affectu*) that excludes the existence or presence of that body.'

[150] *Ethics* V, 7 Dem.; CWS I, 600.

[151] I agree with Jean-Marie Beyssade's conclusions on this point. Ibid., p. 123.

Second, the adverbial phrase '*et simul*' in Definition 3 of *Ethics* III cannot take on not only a conjunctive meaning but a distributive one as well. It can refer to mind and body together, or at times to one and at times to the other. Saying that affect is at the same time an affection of the body, the idea of this affection is therefore an invitation to conceptualise it as a reality where corporeal and intellectual states are understood either simultaneously or separately, given that they always have a correlate and that all affects of the body correspond to an idea and all affects of the mind to a determination of the body. Just like affections, affects can give rise to three types of discourse: psychophysical, mental or physical, depending on whether they are related at the same time to the mind and the body, to the mind alone or to the body alone. Nevertheless, it is not enough to pinpoint the presence of the term *affectus* applied to the body; we must also identify the nature of this type of emotion and its various subtypes. Given that he does not intend to deal with the body *ex professo*,[152] Spinoza does not say much on the subject. It is, then, a question of finding out what the three categories of affect refer to, and determining their respective spheres.

---

[152] Cf. *Ethics* II, 13 Schol.; CWS I, 457–8.

5

Variations of the Mixed Discourse

The Three Categories of Affect: Mental, Physical and Psychophysical

Establishing a typology of affects according to their constituting principle and the relationship they have with mind and body appears, at first glance, to be a pointless and arduous undertaking. It is pointless because Spinoza does not engage in this type of inventorying exercise. Above all, he draws three main distinctions with regard to affects: between actions and passions, between primitive affects and combinations of them, and between good and bad, according to their effect on the power of acting. It is arduous because it would be impossible to review all the physical, mental and psychophysical affects, given that listing them would be endless since there can be infinite combinations of emotions within *natura naturata*.

Spinoza, however, does not reject the principle of differentiating the affects according to their relationship with mind and body, since he uses it to justify his omission of the definitions of cheerfulness, pleasure, melancholy and pain.[1] He does not trouble himself either with the false problem of a comprehensive list, because his aim is not so much a complete as a sufficient inventory of the affects. Without naming them one by one, he nevertheless covers all the affects since, despite their limitless number and specific characters, he knows that they all boil down to kinds of

[1] Cf. *Ethics* III, DA 3 Exp.; CWS I, 532.

desire, joy or sadness. That is why, following Spinoza's example, it is not a question of drawing a complete picture but, rather, of identifying whether an affect is physical, mental or psychophysical according to the dominant or equivalent role mind and body play in its formation. To that end, it is a good idea to follow Spinoza's classification system and use the three affects he calls 'primitive, or primary' (*primitivos, seu primarios*),[2] to understand how all the other affects are generated and their relationship to the mind or the body. On this basis, it is possible first to distinguish the affects expressly related to both.

Psychophysical Affects

This includes not only desire, which is conscious appetite,[3] but also all the primitive affects, at least as they are defined at the end of Part III of the *Ethics*. Joy and sadness are in fact represented, respectively, as *man*'s passage from a lesser to a greater perfection and from a greater to a lesser perfection.[4] Yet man is explicitly defined as a being 'consist[ing] of a Mind and a Body',[5] such that the use of this term, as in Descartes, refers to the union of a thinking thing and an extended thing and invites us to think of them in concert. In this case, affect is a psychophysical reality and is the object of a mixed discourse expressing mind and body on a par with each other.

Besides the primitive triad of affects, this category contains derived affects, such as pride or humility, which are related to man and involve both a physical and mental state. While 'Humility is a Sadness born of the fact that a man considers his own lack of power or weakness',[6] pride is related to 'thinking more highly of oneself than is just'.[7] The proud person 'is anxious to tell his own deeds and show off his powers, both of body and of mind',[8] while

---

[2] Cf. *Ethics* III, DA 4 Exp.; CWS I, 532.
[3] *Ethics* III, 9 Schol.; CWS I, 500.
[4] Cf. *Ethics* III, DA 2 and 3; CWS I, 531–2.
[5] *Ethics* II, 13 Cor.; CWS I, 457.
[6] *Ethics* III, DA 26; CWS I, 536.
[7] *Ethics* III, DA 28; CWS I, 537.
[8] *Ethics* III, 55 Schol.; CWS I, 525.

humble people sadly confess their physical and mental weakness. These two passions produce effects at once psychological and physiological, and are accompanied by common behaviours allowing the observer to identify and catalogue the people affected by them.

> For we usually call him proud who exults too much at being esteemed (see 30S), who tells of nothing but his own virtues and the vices of others, who wishes to be given precedence over all others, and finally who proceeds with the gravity and attire usually adopted by others who are placed far above him. On the other hand, we call him humble who quite often blushes, who confesses his own vices and tells the virtues of others, who yields to all, and finally, who walks with head bowed, and neglects to adorn himself.[9]

Admittedly, these manifestations concern their effects rather than their nature.[10] They fall more under an agreed-upon description of these affects than a genuine conception of their essence, so much so that Spinoza will show that pride is not, as one would believe on the basis of observing behavioural reactions, the opposite of humility, but rather of despondency. Furthermore, some physical symptoms, such as blushing, bowing one's head or holding it arrogantly high, are similar to these insignificant external affections such as paleness or sobbing. In the case of humility or pride, however, these secondary affections combining bodily and intellectual signs are worthy of attention, since they indicate and illustrate the psychophysical nature of these affects.

But if these three primitive affects are simultaneously related to the mind and the body, it would appear obvious as a result that all the other affects involve this double relationship, since they are all combinations of them. However, although the primitive affects are formed by an affection of the body and an idea of this affection, they can nevertheless be characterised either primarily by the affection of the body or primarily by the idea of

---

[9] *Ethics* III, DA 29 Exp.; CWS I, 538.
[10] Cf. Ibid.

this affection. The powers of thinking and acting being equal do not exclude the salience of the mental or physical aspect of the affect. Thus, for example, the fact that joy and sadness involve both mind and body – in that they convey the variations of perfection in people – in no way prevents Spinoza from considering their mental aspect to be primary: quite the contrary. This is demonstrated by the fact that in the first definitions that he gives of them (and which are valid for all of Part III except the last two propositions devoted to active affects), he groups them with the passions through which the *mind* – and not *the person* – passes to a greater or lesser perfection.[11] The body is never expressly mentioned. Joy and sadness are, above all, mental phenomena here, so much so that when Spinoza wants to relate these affects to the mind and the body at the same time, he changes their names: 'The affect of Joy which is related to the Mind and Body at once (*simul relatum*) I call Pleasure or Cheerfulness, and that of Sadness, Pain or Melancholy.'[12]

But here again the expression '*simul relatum*' should not mislead us, because it is clear that these four affects – pleasure and pain, which 'are ascribed to a man when one part of him is affected more than the rest',[13] as well as cheerfulness and melancholy, which 'are ascribed to him when all are equally affected',[14] – concern the body above all. Spinoza later says it expressly in the explanation of Definition 3 of the Affects. Moreover, it is also the reason why he refuses to analyse them further, seeing that his account focuses on analysing the passions of the mind and the obstacles to its power: 'As for the definitions of Cheerfulness, Pleasure, Melancholy, and Pain, I omit them, because they are chiefly related to the Body (*ad corpus potissimum referentur*).' The adverb '*potissimus*' means 'chiefly', 'most of all' or 'preferably'. Shirley and Curley translate it as 'chiefly'; Caillois and Pautrat choose to translate it

---

[11] Cf. *Ethics* III, 11 Schol.; *CWS* I, 500–1: 'By *Joy*, therefore, I shall understand in what follows that *passion by which the Mind passes to a greater perfection*. And by *Sadness*, that *passion by which it passes to a lesser perfection*.'

[12] Ibid.

[13] Ibid.

[14] Ibid.

into French as '*principalement*' ('chiefly'), Appuhn as '*éminemment*' ('eminently'), but in each case it is clear that it indicates that the body is predominant.

Bodily Affects

Does this mean that melancholy, cheerfulness, pleasure and pain are part of these much vaunted bodily affects that Spinoza alludes to in general, without naming them or going into detail about them? The key question is whether the adverb *potissimus* indicates a simple preference or whether it means that the body is the cause of these affects. Can we go from the fact that they are mainly ascribed to the body to the fact that they are ascribed to the body, period? In other words, can we do without the adverb *potissimus*? In any case, Spinoza does indeed dispense with it, since in the demonstrations of Propositions 42 and 43 of *Ethics* IV, he presents cheerfulness and pleasure as joy and melancholy and pain as sadness, related to the body, while omitting the adverb 'chiefly'.[15] This lexical clue argues in favour of the affects having a bodily status, but is not sufficient to establish it. To do this, one must show that these kinds of joy and sadness satisfy the conditions required to be affects of the body. For this point of view there can be no doubt about this, since they have an impact on the body's power of acting and modulate it according to the four characteristic modes of increasing, decreasing, aiding and constraining. Cheerfulness is among the affections through which 'the Body's power of acting is increased or aided, so that all its parts maintain the same proportion of motion and rest to one another'.[16] Through melancholy, on the other hand, 'the Body's power of

---

[15] *Ethics* IV, 42 Dem.; CWS I, 570: 'Cheerfulness [. . .] is a Joy which, insofar as it is related to the Body, consists in this, that all parts of the Body are equally affected [. . .] But Melancholy [. . .] is a sadness, which, insofar as it is related to the Body, consists in this, that the Body's power of acting is absolutely diminished or constrained.' Translation modified. *Ethics* IV, 43 Dem.; CWS I, 570: 'Pleasure is a Joy which, insofar as it is related to the Body, consists in this, that one (or several) of its parts are affected more than the others.'

[16] *Ethics* IV, 42 Dem.; CWS I, 570.

acting is absolutely diminished or constrained'.[17] Pleasure and pain also feature among the affections that weaken the body's power of acting, but their status is more ambiguous. Depending on whether it is moderate or excessive, pleasure can in turn belong to the categories of affects that are favourable or unfavourable to the power of acting.[18] While pain generally curbs the power of acting, it can sometimes come to its aid, if it is the kind that 'can constrain Pleasure, so that it is not excessive'.[19]

Although the mind certainly has an idea of them, these four affects are undeniably affects of the body, since they involve modifications that concern that structure of movement and rest that defines it and express a balance or imbalance between its parts, depending on whether or not they are equally affected. They are therefore formed at the level of extension, originate in this attribute, and convey the variations of the body's power of acting. Even though Spinoza does not linger over their definition, affects of the body are no less common than their mental counterparts. If cheerfulness 'is more easily conceived than observed',[20] as it is true that all parts of the body are rarely affected by joy equally and at the same time, pleasure, on the other hand, is so commonplace that it is the most frequently encountered joyous affect in humans. Indeed, in Chapter 30 of the Appendix to Part IV, Spinoza observes that 'Joy is generally related particularly to one part of the body'. Far from being rare, the affects of the body titillate and obsess us, so much so that the mind fixates on a single object as a result.[21]

In the category of affects related to the body, we can also find disgust, or the boredom that arises from a state of being physically sated. Indeed, Spinoza explains the weariness resulting from

[17] Ibid.
[18] Cf. Ethics IV, 43; CWS I, 570.
[19] Ethics IV, 43 Dem.; CWS I, 571. Translation modified.
[20] Ethics IV, 44 Schol.; CWS I, 571.
[21] Cf. Ethics IV, 44 Schol.; CWS I, 571: 'For the affects by which we are daily torn are generally related to a part of the Body which is affected more than the others. Generally, then, the affects are excessive, and occupy the Mind in the consideration of only one object so much that it cannot think of others.'

enjoyment by bodily modifications, so that our loves arise or come to an end depending on whether the body is voracious or full.

> Nevertheless, this remains to be noted about Love: very often it happens that while we are enjoying a thing we wanted, the Body acquires from this enjoyment a new constitution (*constitutio*), by which it is differently determined, and other images of things are aroused in it; and at the same time the Mind begins to imagine other things and desire other things. For example, when we imagine something that usually pleases us by its taste, we desire to enjoy it – that is, to consume it. But while we thus enjoy it, the stomach is filled and the Body constituted differently. So if (while the Body is now differently disposed) the presence of the food or drink encourages the image of it, and consequently also the striving, or Desire, to consume it, then that new constitution will be opposed to this Desire, or striving. Hence, the presence of the food or drink we used to want will be hateful. This is what we call Disgust and Weariness (*fastidium* and *tedium*).[22]

Disgust and weariness therefore result from a bodily change and express revulsion towards a thing that has become odious as a result of the body becoming satiated. They combine desire and love that have become a present hatred by adopting the body's successive transformations. On this point, Spinoza agrees with Descartes, for whom disgust is above all a bodily essence, explained by a change in appetite and the transformation of something pleasant into something disagreeable.[23] The physiological origin of disgust and weariness is doubtlessly the reason why Spinoza does not return to them in his final definitions of the affects, ignoring them, as he does cheerfulness and melancholy.

[22] *Ethics* III, 59 Schol.; CWS I, 530.
[23] Cf. *Passions of the Soul* CCVIII: 'Disgust is a kind of sadness that results from the same cause as that from which joy came previously. For we are so constituted that most of the things we enjoy are good for us only for a time, and afterwards become disagreeable. This is evident especially in the case of drinking and eating, which are beneficial only so long as we have an appetite, and harmful when we no longer have one. Because such things then cease to be agreeable to our taste, this passion is called "disgust".'

Mental Affects

The affects of the body have as their counterparts the affects of the mind, which Spinoza seems to spend more time on, as he focuses on the mental aspect. Nevertheless, it is not an easy task to determine which emotions fall strictly into the area of thought. Indeed, the primitive affects of joy and sadness, defined in Part III as either the mind's passions [24] or actions[25] – at least as far as joy is concerned – are finally ascribed to humans[26] and also involve the body. In any event, it is undeniable that some affects, such as the satisfaction of the mind (*mentis acquiescientia*) and the intellectual love of God, belong in the category of mental affects, since they arise from the third kind of knowledge[27] and are related to the mind without relating to the present existence of the body.

Glory is also connected to the realm of mental affects. Whether it is an action equivalent to satisfaction of mind[28] or a joyous passion related to 'the idea of some action of ours which we imagine that others praise',[29] it arises from a mental representation of ourselves and is based on an adequate or inadequate perception of our own perfection. In general, affects related to the mind are caused by an idea, a decision, a desire or another mode of thinking. Thus, for example, repentance (*penitentia*) is above all a mental passion, since it 'is a Sadness accompanied by the idea of some deed we believe ourselves to have done from a free decision of the Mind'.[30] In this it is different from longing (*desiderium*), which involves a relationship both to the mind and body, in that it 'is a Desire, or Appetite, to possess something which is encouraged by

---

[24] Cf. *Ethics* III, 11 Schol.; *CWS* I, 500–1.
[25] Cf. *Ethics* III, 59; *CWS* I, 529.
[26] Cf. *Ethics* III, DA 2 and 3; *CWS* I, 531.
[27] *Ethics* V, 27; *CWS* I, 609: 'The greatest satisfaction of mind there can be arises from this third kind of knowledge' and *Ethics* V, 32 Cor.; *CWS* I, 611: 'From the third kind of knowledge, there necessarily arises an intellectual love of God.'
[28] Cf. *Ethics* V, 36 Schol.; *CWS* I, 612–13, where these two affects are equivalent.
[29] *Ethics* III, DA 30; *CWS* I, 538.
[30] *Ethics* III, DA 27; *CWS* I, 536–7.

the memory of that thing, and at the same time restrained by the memory of other things which exclude the existence of the thing wanted'.[31]

Variations of the Mixed Discourse

Although there are not only affects of mind *and* body but also affects of mind *or* body, we must not accentuate the difference between the two and think that the mixed discourse boils down to a long physical or mental monologue. In reality, all discourse on the affects always has a psychophysical essence to a certain extent. Although cheerfulness, melancholy, pleasure and pain are rooted in the body, they are necessarily accompanied by mental repercussions, such that the physical discourse on the affects does not exclude considerations on the mind but integrates them as correlates. Indeed, 'the idea of any thing that increases or diminishes, aids or constrains our Body's power of acting, increases or diminishes, aids or constrains our Mind's power of thinking'.[32] By the same token, cheerfulness or melancholy necessarily comes with mental joy or sadness. That is why the discourse regarding the body's affects is always mixed. Mental by-products are added on top of its mainly physical nature. This helps us understand why Spinoza makes flexible use of the concepts of cheerfulness, melancholy, pleasure and pain, by relating them to the mind and body, in turn, in the Scholium to Proposition 11 of Part III, then mainly to the body in the explanation of Definition 3. There is no inconsistency here, since, although these affects originate in the body, the mind feels their fallout, and its power of acting is modified in either a joyous or a sad direction. Consequently, anyone who considers only how they are formed will relate them to the body, whereas anyone who looks at the matter in terms of the power of acting of the person as a whole will relate them to the mind and body. Conversely, mental affects do not completely disregard the body. However much actions, such as the intellectual love of God or satisfaction of mind, try to exclude

---

[31] *Ethics* III, DA 32; CWS I, 539.
[32] *Ethics* III, 11; CWS I, 500. Translation modified.

any reference to the current, present existence of the body, they still imply a relationship with it, since the mind remains an idea expressing the essence of the body under a species of eternity.[33] However much passions, such as repentance, are connected to the idea of a bad deed that we believe we have done by free decree, they can only be understood and overcome by updating the bodily mechanism underpinning them without our knowledge. This is what emerges in the Scholium to Proposition 2 of Part III, where Spinoza denounces the illusion of free will and shows 'that we can do nothing from a decision of the Mind unless we recollect it. For example, we cannot speak a word unless we recollect it.' Since recollection involves memory, namely 'a certain connection of ideas involving the nature of things which are outside the human Body – a connection which is in the Mind according to the order and connection of the affections of the human Body',[34] it depends on the preservation of bodily traces of objects. There is no repentance without memory or memory without the excitation of an image. That is why Spinoza concludes that 'the decisions of the Mind are nothing but the appetites themselves, which therefore vary as the disposition of the Body varies'.[35]

In addition, whether they are physical or mental, emotions do not have intrinsically different natures, and require neither the separation of physiological from psychological analyses nor the formation of specialized discourses. Spinoza explains that affects 'all arise from Desire, Joy or Sadness or *rather, that they are nothing but these three*,[36] each one generally being called by a different name on account of its varying relations and extrinsic denominations'.[37] The many kinds of desire, joy and sadness are differentiated more in name than in fact, since their essence is fundamentally the same, but it is explained and named differently according to the objects it refers to. 'The names of the affects

[33] Cf. *Ethics* V, 22 and 23; CWS I, 607.
[34] *Ethics* II, 18 Schol.; CWS I, 465–6.
[35] *Ethics* III, 2 Schol.; CWS I, 496–7.
[36] Emphasis added.
[37] *Ethics* III, DA 48 Exp.; CWS I, 541.

are guided more by usage than by nature',[38] Spinoza points out. Indeed, the principle of naming and specification is based less on differing natures than on the variety of relationships to their objects.[39] Thus, for example:

> Gluttony, Drunkenness, Lust, Greed and Ambition, which are only notions of Love or Desire, explain the nature of each of these affects through the objects to which they are related. For by Gluttony, Drunkenness, Lust, Greed and Ambition we understand nothing but an immoderate Love or Desire for eating, drinking, sexual union, wealth and esteem.[40]

Although emotions, in their infinite diversity, can be reduced to a combination or a derivation of desire, joy or sadness, and only form variations of this primary triad, we must note that their specification and naming are not carried out solely with respect to external objects but also with regard to the principal relationship with the mind or the body. The reference to the mind or the body serves as a criterion of differentiation and as a principle of identification. The unity of naming makes way for a variety of designations, depending on whether the angle of analysis is physical or mental. The term 'joy' is mostly reserved for the mind, to the point of being defined only in relation to it in the Scholium to Proposition 11 of Ethics III, while the terms 'cheerfulness' and 'melancholy' refer to the body. These names may well be extrinsic, since mind and body are one and the same thing, but they are not arbitrary and baseless, since they refer to the constitutive principle of affect, depending on whether it relates more to mind or body and involves thought or extension.

The best-known case is how the name of the love that a human being, who understands himself clearly and distinctly, feels toward

---

[38] Ethics III, DA 31 Exp.; CWS I, 538–9.

[39] Cf. Ethics III, 56; CWS I, 526: 'There are as many species of Joy, Sadness and Desire, and consequently of each affect composed of these (like vacillation of mind) or derived from them (like Love, Hate, Hope, Fear, etc.), as there are species of objects by which we are affected.'

[40] Ethics III, 56 Schol.; CWS I, 527.

God, changes. This love is called 'love towards God' (*amor erga Deum*), when related to the mind in connection with the body, and the 'intellectual love of God' when related to the mind alone. The vocabulary, while demonstrating the equality between the mind's power of thinking and the body's power of acting, stops us from conceiving it as uniform and undifferentiated, since it introduces nuances in the expression of this love that is one and the same, depending on which of the two different attributes it is considered under. This variation in formulation, according to whether the relationship is with the mind or the body, is based on an extrinsic designation, like all the names given to the affects, but it nevertheless reflects an intrinsic difference, since the nature of this love changes according to the angle from which it is considered. *Amor erga Deum* and *amor intellectualis* admittedly have in common the fact that they are both kinds of love, but the first is related to God 'insofar as we imagine him as present',[41] while the second affects the mind 'insofar as we understand God to be eternal'.[42] The first varies according to how the presence of God is imagined, while the other is based on an adequate conception of his eternity. This difference regarding the mode of representation of the cause is not irrelevant, since it reflects on the essence of this love, depending on whether it is related to the mind or the body. This is what Spinoza highlights when he maintains that the love toward God is

> the most constant of all the affects and, insofar as it is related to the Body, cannot be destroyed, unless it is destroyed with the Body itself. What the nature of this Love is insofar as it is related only to the Mind, we shall see later.[43]

He later explains this nature in Proposition 33 of *Ethics* V, where he shows that the intellectual love of God is eternal, and that it is the only love to boast of this property. The affect of the intellectual love of God therefore differs in nature depending on whether

---

[41] *Ethics* V, 32 Cor.; CWS I, 611.
[42] Ibid.
[43] *Ethics* V, 20 Schol.; CWS I, 605.

it is related to the body or the mind. When related to the body, it is characterised by its constancy, when related to the mind, by its eternity. 'Love towards God' is temporal and temporary. It dies with the body. 'Intellectual love' is atemporal and eternal; it remains with the mind. The discourse on the love of God therefore accepts variation, according to whether it is related to the mind or the body.

Consequently, although the order and connection of the ideas of the affections is the same as the order and connection of the body's affections, this does not mean that all affects concern the mind and body in the same way. Each of them has a specificity so that one can be more involved than the other. Although an affect has two sides, they are not uniform; its physical and mental aspects do not always have the same importance and do not overlap on a one-to-one basis according to a correspondence. The same affect can have a different impact and varying effects, depending on whether the angle of analysis under which it is conceived is more physical, mental, or psychophysical. Self-satisfaction (*acquiescentia in se ipso*), for example, involves both mind and body, because it is defined as 'a Joy born of the fact that a man considers himself and his own power of acting'[44] and therefore refers as much to a physical as a mental force. However, depending on whether its psychophysical or only its mental nature is stressed, it does not have the same opposites and consequently the same effects. Self-satisfaction is

> opposed to Humility, insofar as we understand by it a Joy born of the fact that we consider our power of acting. But insofar as we also understand by it a Joy, accompanied by the idea of some deed that we believe we have done from a free decision of the Mind, it is opposed to Repentance.[45]

In the first case, this affect is contrasted with an antagonistic affect, humility, yet one with a similar psychophysical nature. Self-satisfaction contrasts a joy that emanates from the representation

---

[44] *Ethics* III, DA 25; CWS I, 536.
[45] *Ethics* III, DA 26 Exp.; CWS I, 536.

of one's physical or mental power with 'a Sadness born of the fact that a man considers his own lack of power, or weakness'.[46] In the second case, self-satisfaction takes on a more mental hue, since it refers to the idea that we have freely made the right decision to act. It is not an antidote to humility, seeing that it does not in any way thwart our physical weaknesses, but rather to repentance, the mental passion linked to the representation 'of some deed we believe ourselves to have done from a free decision of the Mind'. Spinoza's monism is therefore far from being black and white; he allows for nuances in the emotions depending on whether they are conceived *sub specie corporis* or *sub specie mentis*.

That is why the correlation between a bodily affection and the idea of this affection, expressed by the adverbial phrase '*et simul*' in Definition 3, cannot be reduced to a system of parallels. Mind and body are affected at the same time without necessarily having the same tempo. Their synchrony is not at all linear, nor does it take the systematic and mechanical form of an identical replication. The phrase '*et simul*' can therefore take on at least three different meanings. Firstly, it can refer to the mind and body at the same time, and on a par. Secondly, it can refer mainly to the mind. Thirdly, it can refer mainly to the body.

These meanings are not completely closed off and rigid, since a mixed discourse implies differences of degree and expresses all the nuances of a palette, ranging from the principal and fundamental reference to the mind moved by the intellectual love of God, to the body titillated by pleasure or tortured by pain, with intermediate affects that mobilise one of them more or less than the other situated between the two extremes. Thus a certain number of affects that are kinds of desire and love, such as gluttony (*luxuria*), drunkenness (*ebrietas*), greed (*avaritia*) or lust (*libido*) are differentiated not only according to their objects but also according to the manner in which they involve mind and body. It is obvious that they are defined first and foremost in relation to the body and its needs: gluttony, 'an immoderate desire for and love of eating',[47] drunkenness, 'an immoderate desire for

---

[46] *Ethics* III, DA 26.
[47] *Ethics* III, DA 45; CWS I, 541.

and love of drinking',[48] greed, 'an immoderate desire for and love of wealth'[49] and, lastly, lust, 'a desire for and love of joining one body to another'.[50] However, they do not have the same status as melancholy, cheerfulness, pleasure and pain, since they are not expressly defined as relating chiefly to the body. The proof is that they are subject to a separate, independent definition at the end of Part III, while the four affects obviously related to the body are deliberately omitted or ignored. This difference in treatment is due to the fact that these affects go beyond their physical manifestations and their essence is not purely corporeal. Spinoza lets it be understood clearly in the explanation of lust that 'absolutely, these affects do not so much concern the acts of eating, drinking and so forth, as the appetite itself and the love'. They therefore express a human desire that exceeds bodily determinations. The body, nevertheless, seems to be more involved than in the affects defined previously, such as ambition or human kindness. Indeed, 'an excessive desire for esteem'[51] or 'a desire to do what pleases men and not do what displeases them'[52] mobilises the mind more.

The examples of gluttony, drunkenness, greed and lust reveal the complexity of the emotions and, when the starting point is the unity of mind and body, it is difficult to untangle the part played by each in the formation of affects. It invites us to break with the simplistic conception of equality between the powers of thinking and acting, which would make it the result of analogous activity in the mind and in the body or the identical reflection of what happens in each of the modes. It is not a question of being fooled by appearances, but rather of determining what principle is operating in the affect, regardless of its mental or physical hue.

Thus, for example, passions such as pity or envy, which would appear to reflect the state of mind of a person who tends to inflict the misfortune of others on himself or to be jealous of others' happiness, are actually rooted in the body, because they are based on

[48] *Ethics* III, DA 46; CWS I, 541.
[49] *Ethics* III, DA 47; CWS I, 541.
[50] *Ethics* III, DA 48; CWS I, 541–2.
[51] *Ethics* III, DA 44; CWS I, 541.
[52] *Ethics* III, DA 43; CWS I, 541.

affective imitation and arise from the fact that we observe others laughing or crying. That is what emerges from the Scholium to Proposition 32 of *Ethics* III. Experience shows us that, starting from childhood, people 'pity the unfortunate and envy the fortunate'[53] because of their tendency to imitate others' behaviour:

> For we find from experience that children, because their bodies are continually, as it were, in a state of equilibrium, laugh or cry simply because they see others laugh or cry. Moreover, whatever they see others do, they immediately desire to imitate it. And finally, they desire for themselves all those things by which they imagine others are pleased.[54]

This mimicking behaviour falls under physical determinations, since it is caused by the images of things that are 'affections of the human Body, or modes by which the human Body is affected by external causes, and disposed to do this or that'.[55]

The imitation of affects is first and foremost a bodily phenomenon and involves observing others' behaviour and reproducing it spontaneously without thinking. It can give rise to a whole range of affects, such as pity or emulation, depending on whether it is related to sadness or desire,[56] and then be accompanied by mental representations. Emulation, which 'is nothing but the Desire for a thing which is generated in us from the fact that we imagine others like us to have the same Desire',[57] cannot be reduced to pure physical mimicry. It involves a judgement regarding the value of what is being imitated, and consequently draws upon the mind. That is what emerges from Definition 33.

> If someone flees because he sees others flee, or is timid because he sees others timid or, because he sees that someone else has burned his hand, withdraws his own hand and moves his body as if his hand were burned, we shall say that he imitates the

---

[53] *Ethics* III, 32 Schol.; CWS I, 513.
[54] Ibid.
[55] Ibid.
[56] Cf. *Ethics* III, 27 Schol.; CWS I, 509.
[57] Ibid.

other's affect, but not that he emulates it – not because we know that emulation has one cause and imitation another, but because it has come about by usage that we call emulous only one who imitates what we judge to be honourable, useful or pleasant.

In Spinoza's eyes, imitation and emulation do not have different causes but the second adds to the first the conscious desire to do the same, in ourselves as well as in others, as those to whom we attribute the same frame of mind. Emulation is therefore not solely based on a bodily determination but on a presumed or real wish to do the right thing, and it takes us into the mental sphere of consciousness and intentions. It is doubtlessly the reason why it is the subject of a proper definition in the final collection, while the imitation of affects – which is, after all, the keystone of relationships between fellow human beings and of their affective lives – is left out and appears only as a side note in the explanations. This lack of a final definition of the imitation of affects probably stems from the fact that it mainly concerns the body, its behaviour and reflexes, as the examples of fleeing, fear and the burned hand demonstrate. It therefore has a status analogous to cheerfulness's or melancholy's and is not mentioned for the same reasons.

Far from taking on the shape of a strict parallelism, equality between the powers of thinking and acting takes very diverse forms. Spinoza highlights what happens in the body and the mind in turn, and sometimes introduces an asymmetry that cannot be expressed by the idea of a parallel. This alternating discourse is intended to present only what is essential to master the affects and achieve beatitude. It is important to identify the cases where analysis of the body is crucial from cases where it is superfluous. Although external affections of the body, such as blushing, pallor or sobbing can be overlooked, since they are unhelpful in understanding the affects, it is important to highlight the body's spontaneous movements and determinations in order to understand that our decisions and emotions do not result from free will but rather depend on the structure of the body. While proclaiming the unity and identity of mind and body, Spinoza's philosophy considers their differences in expression through the theory of the affects. It also conceptualises the powers of thinking and acting as equal: asserting the primacy of the mind while making the body the primary object of knowledge.

Conclusion

The human understanding from its own peculiar nature willingly
supposes a greater order and regularity in things than it finds, and
though there are many things in nature which are unique and full
of disparities, it invents parallels and correspondences and non-ex-
istent connections.

Francis Bacon, *The New Organon*

When all is said and done, which model of the mind–body relationship emerges from an examination of Spinoza's conception
of the affects? Exploring how the power of acting operates in the
affects has made it possible to show how the psychophysical union
varies, and reconciles a similarity of order and principle with the
mind and body's autonomy of expression. The first point therefore
is to stop searching for any interaction, influence or reciprocal
causality between the mind and the body, and to think of them
only in terms of correspondence and correlation.

From this perspective, the American neurologist Antonio
Damasio was right in maintaining that in Spinoza 'in a strict sense,
the mind did not cause the body and the body did not cause the
mind'.[1] However, Damasio is not always worthy of his model and
sometimes lacks rigour, since he continues to talk about the mind
arising from the body and going from the neural to the mental
level,[2] which Spinoza could not have accepted. It is true that

---

[1] *Looking for Spinoza*, p. 209.
[2] Cf. *Looking for Spinoza*, p. 191: 'It requires an understanding that the mind

it is naturally very difficult to do without the categories of cause and reciprocal action when conceptualising the mind–body relationship, and it is tempting to bring them back in another guise. In this respect, meditating on Spinoza's model is an excellent safeguard against attempts to establish a relationship on the basis of an interaction or influence model, which would always retain its 'occult' qualities.

Although Spinoza's model excludes interaction in favour of correlation, it cannot be reduced for all that to an interplay of parallels between mind and body that express the same thing under two different attributes. This is the second point to make from studying the affects. Spinoza's model of the psychophysical union is not based on parallelism but on equivalence. This equivalence is not uniformity, since it cannot be reduced to echoing the same thing and to mechanical repetition. Indeed, examining the affects casts a reflective light on the doctrine of expression by showing that it is by no means an identical copy of the modes of extension and thought, but exhibits the richness and the variety of the powers within each attribute. We must therefore resist the mind's ingrained tendency to see symmetries and parallels everywhere, as Bacon reminds us. Although the mind is not pre-eminent over the body, there are nevertheless priorities that explain that each of these modes of expression takes centre stage in turn, shining a spotlight on human nature. Far from being monolithic, the mixed discourse arising from the study of the affects takes a multiplicity of forms, expressing variations in the relationship between mind and body according to how they take turns playing a dominant or equal role with respect to each other in the formation of various affects. The much-vaunted equality between humanity's powers of thinking and acting therefore paradoxically allows unequal treatment of the mind and the body, depending on the constitutive principle of the affects.

Although Antonio Damasio was right to highlight that in Spinoza the unity of mind and body does not mean reducing one

arises from or in a brain situated within a body-proper with which it interacts; that due to the mediation of the brain, the mind is grounded in the body-proper.' Cf. also p. 325, note 21.

to the other but, rather, that it preserves a difference of expression, he was wrong to present it in the form of a parallelism. To be fair, he is not the only one to have incorrectly imported this model into Spinoza's philosophy. Moreover, we must put his error into perspective since, although he had noted the similarity between mind and body, Damasio forgets the parallelistic model to show that in Spinoza priority of expression is given to mind and body in turn, according to the nature of the affects: 'The equal footing of mind and body only works in the general description [. . .] Spinoza does not hesitate to privilege body or mind in certain circumstances.'[3] Admittedly, Damasio tends to give primacy to the body and sometimes gives in to the reductionist temptation, all the while denying it. Nevertheless, he has perceived the variations in the discourse and in priority that a parallelistic model would not be able to render.

What remains, then, of the doctrine of 'psychophysical parallelism' that commentators wrongly attribute to Spinoza? The core of positivity that is left after critiquing this false conception lies essentially in the existence of a necessary correlation between the objective essence and the formal essence. There is no question that an idea objectively contains everything that its object contains formally, according to the same order and the same connection. This is true both for the idea of God and for the ideas of the human body and of anything else. Nevertheless, examining the union of mind and body through the prism of the affects reveals that the relationship between an idea and its object takes a more complex form than the parallelism model suggests. The identity of the order and the connection between ideas and things should not mask the difference in expression specific to the modes of each attribute. The surreptitious shift, from asserting the identity of the order to asserting the identity of the modes that follow one another other according to the same connection, is probably largely responsible for the improper extension of the parallelism doctrine and its succession of errors. Although only one thing exists that produces effects according to a single causal order, it is nevertheless expressed in an infinite number of ways in

---

[3] *Looking for Spinoza*, p. 214.

the case of God, and in two ways in the case of humankind. This is why the relationship between the idea and the object obeys the logic of both identity and difference, which Spinoza returns to in the concept of equality. Although it is never explicitly defined in the *Ethics*, this concept plays a key role in making it possible to reconcile the one and the many, and it conveys the relationship between the various expressions related to the common standard of the same thing. Since Spinoza's intellect is the power of truth, all that remains therefore is to tickle the spiritual automaton with adequate ideas in order to break away from a perfunctory parallelism, and instead promote an expressive equality of the mind and the body's modal diversity.

It would no doubt have been interesting to broaden this model of equality and shed more light on the relationship between idea and object, by extending the investigations on the essence of the affects to examining how they are expressed in the body politic and constitute it as an individual, following the example of human beings. The State, as the body politic, does indeed experience affects, be they passive, such as hope[4] and fear[5], or active when they follow reason.[6] Thus, for example, alliances between States are mainly based on two motives: 'the fear of loss or hope of profit'.[7] 'But if either body politic loses its hope or fear, it is left dependent on its own right',[8] so the bond of obligation linking them together is broken. Consequently, if a State experiences affects, an analysis of the body politic should make it possible to read in large letters, to use Plato's metaphor, what the human body writes in small letters, and what half-blind experience has not yet made it possible to decipher.

It remains to be seen, however, whether examining the nature of the State's affects and studying the correlation between the body politic and its mind, can truly shed new light on the psychophysical union. The legitimacy of conclusions on this subject

---

[4] Cf. *TP* III, 14; *CWS* II, 523.
[5] Cf. *TP* III, 9; *CWS* II, 521 and III, 12; *CWS* II, 522–3.
[6] *TP* III, 14; *CWS* II, 523.
[7] Ibid.
[8] Ibid. Translation modified.

hinges on the issue of whether, beyond the simple metaphor, it is possible to amalgamate the human individual and the political individual. Although individuality is not specific to humanity, we must beware of the surreptitious return of the prejudices of anthropomorphism and anthropocentrism, which result in tacking the nature of the body politic on to the human body.

Beyond a difference of degree, there is in fact a difference of nature between the constitution of the human individual and the State. That, at least, is what Spinoza's problematic wording on the subject suggests. While a person consists of a mind and a body, according to the corollary to Proposition 13 of *Ethics* II, the State has a body and 'something' like a mind. In the *Political Treatise*, in fact, Spinoza does not maintain that in a State people form one mind and one body, but that they *'are led as if by one mind'*.[9] The analogous nature communicated by the expression 'as it were' leaves open the question of whether the State really has a mind or just something resembling it. There is therefore an asymmetry in the wording, suggesting that Spinoza unhesitatingly endows the State with a body but remains more reserved when it comes to attributing a mind to it. Chapter III of the *Political Treatise* corroborates this asymmetry, since the State is equated unconditionally with a body called 'the *civitas*'[10] and obeys the laws of what makes a 'composite individual', as presented after Proposition 13 of *Ethics* II. The body politic is a union of individuals who have reached agreement and pool their resources in order to gain more rights.

[9] Emphasis added. This expression occurs several times:

– in II, 16; CWS II, 514: 'Where men have common rights, and all are led *as if by one mind (omnesque una veluti mente ducuntur)*'.

– in II, 21; CWS II, 515: 'a multitude can't be led *as if by one mind (una veluti mente ducatur)*, as is required in a state . . .'

– in III, 2; CWS II, 517: 'it's evident that the Right of a state, or of the supreme powers, is nothing more than the Right of nature, determined not by the power of each person, but by the power of a multitude, led *as if by one mind (quae una veluti mente ducitur)*. That is, just as each person in the natural state has as much right as he has power, so also the body and mind of the whole state have as much right as they have power.'

– In III, 5; CWS II, 519: 'the body of the state must be guided as if by one mind *(una veluti mente duci)*.'

[10] Cf. *TP* III, 1; CWS II, 517.

The parties of this body are people, who are citizens inasmuch as they enjoy the advantages of the *civitas*, as well as subjects inasmuch as they must obey its laws.[11] Although Spinoza unreservedly assigns a body to the State, he is loath to attribute a mind to it, and limits himself to talking about a quasi-mind constituted by laws and its entire right.[12] The issue therefore is not whether Spinoza really equates the State with the human individual or whether he is simply using an analogy, as he often does, since this angle of analysis wrongly places the mind and body on the same level, whereas they are treated differently. The problem with the analogy concerns only the mind, since it goes without saying that the State has a body. Under these circumstances, the question arises as to the value of the much-vaunted *veluti*, referring to the mind.

The reservation it introduces is unlikely to mean that there is no idea of the body politic, or that the model of how the State is formed is based on a simple analogy with the constitution of the human individual. Rather, it expresses the fact that the term *mens* qualifies more the idea of the human body than that of the body politic. Spinoza appears to be reluctant to use the word 'mind' for individuals other than humans. This is evidenced by the fact that when he proclaims that there is an idea of everything in God, and especially an idea of all bodies, he does not say that all bodies have a mind, but that they are all animate to different degrees.[13] He prefers to talk about 'animate' beings rather than beings 'endowed with a mind'. Describing the State with the expression 'as if by one mind' refers to this reservation, so that the unconditional attribution of a *mens* is done only for humans. This does not

[11] Cf. Ibid.

[12] *TP* IV, 1; CWS II, 525: 'the right of the supreme powers is determined by their power, and we've seen that [that right] consists chiefly in this, that it is, as it were, the mind of the state, by which everyone ought to be guided.'

[13] *Ethics* II, 13 Schol.; CWS I, 458: 'For the things we have shown so far are completely general and do not pertain more to man than to other Individuals, all of which, though in different degrees, are nevertheless animate. For of each thing there is necessarily an idea in God, of which God is the cause in the same way as he is of the idea of the human body. And so, whatever we have said of the idea of the human Body must also be said of the idea of anything.'

invalidate the possibility of research concerning the relationship of equality between the body of the State and its idea, or that of other individuals in nature and their idea, since Spinoza maintains that there are common properties and that 'whatever we have said of the idea of the human Body must also be said of the idea of any thing'.[14] This, however, cannot properly describe the psychophysical union in human beings by rights. Although research on the State's affects can reveal new themes and shed new light on the power of acting, it would not in any case be legitimate to systematically apply the conclusions valid for an individual commonwealth to the psychophysical union and to the relationship between the idea and its object, as they are defined in Part II of the *Ethics*. It is very likely that looking through a magnifying mirror would deform and obscure the union it claims to reveal. That is why it is preferable to limit ourselves to examining the affects in human beings in order to determine the nature of the psychophysical union, and of the equality between the body's power of acting and the mind's power of thinking.

As instant reflections of humanity's power of acting, affects bear witness to its variations and its greater or lesser perfection, depending on whether the cause producing them is adequate or inadequate. Human perfection manifests itself at its highest point through active affects based on reason and intuitive knowledge. By contrast, it is diminished according to the weakness of the body's aptitudes, which reaches its peak in death. While death puts an end to the body's affections, *fortitudo* and its two varieties, firmness and generosity, form the keystone of Spinozan freedom. The mind and the body's power of acting is never as strong as when it takes the form of the love of God, which is an eternal affect.

Thus, the three physical, mental, and psychophysical expressions of the power of acting boil down to variations of this part of eternity that falls to each person in proportion to his striving to persevere in being. As Alain asserts:

The eternal is in each person, and is truly who he is. Try to grasp this power of his, in those happy moments when he is himself,

[14] Ibid.

when he is fully expressed in existence through a happy conflu-
ence of people and things. Fools will say that this happiness is
external to him; but the wise man will perhaps understand that
in these moments of power he is very much himself.[15]

---

[15] *Spinoza*, p. 170: 'Il y a de l'éternel en chacun, et cela c'est proprement lui.
Essayez de saisir cette puissance qui lui est propre, dans ces instants heureux où il est lui-même, où il se traduit tout dans l'existence, par un con-
cours heureux des choses et des hommes. Les sots diront que ce bonheur
lui est extérieur; mais le sage comprendra peut-être qu'à ces moments de
puissance il est hautement lui.'

Bibliography

Primary sources

Bacon, F. [1620] (2000), *The New Organon*, ed. L. Jardine and M. Silverthorne, Cambridge: Cambridge University Press.

Cicero, Marcus Tullius (1945), *Tusculan Disputations*, trans. J. E. King, Cambridge, MA: Harvard University Press.

Descartes, R. (1984–91), *Philosophical Works*, trans. J. Cottingham, R. Stoothoff and D. Murdock, Cambridge: Cambridge University Press.

Descartes, R. (1996), *Œuvres*, ed. C. Adam and P. Tannery, 11 vols, Paris: Librairie philosophique J. Vrin.

Descartes, R. [1637] (2001), *Discourse on Method. Optics, Geometry and Meteorology*, trans. P. J. Olscamp, Indianapolis: Hackett.

Hobbes, T. (1839), 'De Cive', in G. Molesworth (ed.), *Opera philosophica quae latine scripsit omnia in unum corpus nunc primum collecta*, London: Apud Joannem Bohn.

Leibniz, G. W. [1702] (1989), 'Reflections on the Doctrine of a Single Universal Spirit', in *Philosophical Papers and Letters*, trans. and ed. L. E. Loemker, 2nd edn, Dordrecht: Kluwer, p. 556

Ovid (1916), *Metamorphoses. Volume I: Books 1–8*, trans. F. J. Miller, Cambridge, MA: Harvard University Press.

Pappus (1876–8), *Collectionis quae supersunt*, ed. F. Hultsch, Berlin: Waldman.

Princess Elisabeth of Bohemia and R. Descartes (2007), *The Correspondence Between Princess Elisabeth of Bohemia and René*

Descartes, ed. and trans. Lisa Shapiro, Chicago: University of Chicago Press.

Sévigné, Madame de [1675] (2016), *Lettres choisies*, ed. N. Freidel, Paris: Gallimard.

Spinoza, B. (1842), *Œuvres de Spinoza*, trans. É. Saisset, Paris: Charpentier.

Spinoza, B. (1907), *Éthique*, trans. H. de Boulainvilliers, Paris: A. Colin.

Spinoza, B. [1677] (1924), *Opera*, ed. C. Gebhardt, Heidelberg: Carl Winters Universitätsbuchhandlung.

Spinoza, B. (1928), *Œuvres*, trans. C. Appuhn, new revised and corrected edn, Paris: Garnier Frères.

Spinoza, B. (1930), *Éthique*, trans. A. Guérinot, Paris: Éditions d'Art E. Pelletan.

Spinoza, B. (1954), *Éthique*, trans. R. Caillois, Paris: Gallimard.

Spinoza, B. (1988), *Éthique*, trans. B. Pautrat, Paris: Éd. du Seuil.

Spinoza, B. (2005), *Éthique*, trans. R. Misrahi, Paris: Editions de l'éclat.

Spinoza, B. (1985–2016), *The Collected Works*, ed. and trans. E. M. Curley, Princeton: Princeton University Press.

Spinoza, B. (2000), *Ethics*, ed. and trans. G. H. R. Parkinson, Oxford: Oxford University Press.

Spinoza, B. (1992), *Ethics with the Treatise on the Emendation of the Intellect and Selected Letters*, trans. S. Shirley, ed. S. Feldman, Indianapolis: Hackett Publishing Company.

Spinoza, B. [1677] (1955), *The Ethics*, trans. R. Elwes, New York: Dover.

Spinoza, B. (1988), *Etica*, ed. and trans. E. Giancotti, Rome: Editore Riuniti.

Spinoza, B. (2010), *Etica*. ed. and trans. P. Cristofolini, Pisa: Edizioni ETS.

Spinoza, B. (1980), *Ética demostrada según el orden geométrico*, trans. V. Peña Garcia, Madrid: Editora Nacional.

Spinoza, B. (2000), *Ética demostrada según el orden geométrico*. ed. and trans. A. Dominguez, Madrid: Editorial Trotta.

Spinoza B. (1979), *Traité politique*, trans. P.-F. Moreau, Paris: Editions Réplique.

Spinoza, B. (1999), *Tractatus theologico-politicus*, trans. and ed.

P.-F. Moreau and J. Lagrée, Paris: Presses Universitaires de France.

Thomas à Kempis, [1651–9] (1998), *L'Imitation de Jésus-Christ*, trans. P. Corneille, Paris: Albin Michel

Secondary sources

Alain (É. Chartier) [1901] (1986), *Spinoza*, Paris: Éditions Gallimard.

Atlan, H. (2002), *La science est-elle inhumaine?: essai sur la libre nécessité*, Paris: Bayard.

Atlan, H. (2011), *Selected Writings on Self-organization, Philosophy, Bioethics, and Judaism*, ed. Stefanos Geroulanos and Todd Meyers, New York: Fordham University Press, pp. 32–62.

Alquié, F. (1981), *Le rationalisme de Spinoza*, Paris: Presses Universitaires de France.

Ansaldi, S. (2001), *Spinoza et le baroque, infini désir, multitude*, Paris: Kimé.

Bennett, J. (1984), *A Study of Spinoza's Ethics*, Indianapolis: Hackett Publishing.

Beyssade, J.-M. (1990), 'De l'émotion intérieure chez Descartes à l'affect actif spinoziste', in E. Curley and P.-F. Moreau (eds), *Spinoza: Issues and Directions*, Leiden: Brill, pp. 176–90.

Beyssade, J.-M. (1994), 'Sur le mode infini médiat dans l'attribut de la pensée. Du problème (lettre 64) à une solution («*Éthique*» V, 36)', *Revue philosophique de la France et de l'étranger*, 184:1, pp. 23–6.

Bloch, O. (ed.) (1993), *Spinoza au XXe siècle*, Paris: Presses Universitaires de France.

Boss, G. (1982), *L'enseignement de Spinoza. Commentaire du Court Traité*, Zurich: Éditions du Grand Midi.

Bos, H. J. M. (2001), *Redefining Geometrical Exactness: Descartes' Transformation of the Early Modern Concept of Construction*, New York: Springer-Verlag.

Bove, L. (1996), *La stratégie du conatus. Affirmation et résistance chez Spinoza*, Paris: Librairie philosophique J. Vrin.

Bréhier, É. (1968), 'Spinoza', in *Histoire de la philosophie, Tome II. La philosophie moderne*, new edn reviewed and updated by

P.-M. Schuhl, Paris: Presses Universitaires de France, pp. 139–75.

Brugère, F. and P.-F. Moreau (eds) (1998), *Spinoza et les affects*, Paris: Presses de l'Université de Paris-Sorbonne.

Changeux, J.-P. and P. Ricoeur (2000), *What Makes us Think? A Neuroscientist and a Philosopher Argue about Ethics, Human Nature, and the Brain*, trans. M. B. DeBevoise, Princeton: Princeton University Press.

Damasio, A. R. (2003), *Looking for Spinoza: Joy, Sorrow, and the Feeling Brain*, Orlando: Harcourt, Inc. (Fr. tr. *Spinoza avait raison. Joie et tristesse, le cerveau des émotions*, Paris: Odile Jacob.)

Delbos, V. (1926), *Le spinozisme*, Paris: Librairie philosophique J. Vrin.

Delbos, V. [1893] (1990), *Le problème moral dans la philosophie de Spinoza et dans l'histoire du spinozisme*, Paris: Presses de l'Université de Paris-Sorbonne.

Deleuze, G. (1990), *Expressionism in Philosophy: Spinoza*, trans. M. Joughin, New York: Zone Books.

Deleuze, G. (1981), *Spinoza, Philosophie pratique*, Paris: Éditions de Minuit.

Gueroult, M. (1968), *Spinoza 1. Dieu*, Paris: Aubier.

Gueroult, M. (1974), *Spinoza 2. L'âme*, Paris: Aubier.

Israël, N. (2001), *Spinoza. Le temps de la vigilance*, Paris: Payot.

Jaquet, C. (1997a), *Spinoza ou la prudence*, Paris: Quintette.

Jaquet, C. (1997b), *Sub specie aeternitatis. Étude des concepts de temps, durée et éternité chez Spinoza*, Paris: Kimé.

Jaquet, C. (2004), *Les expressions de la puissance d'agir chez Spinoza*. Paris: Publications de la Sorbonne.

Jaquet, C., P. Sévérac and A. Suhamy (eds) (2003), *Fortitude et servitude. Lectures de l'Éthique IV de Spinoza*, Paris: Kimé.

Jaquet, C., P. Sévérac and A. Suhamy (eds) (2005), *Spinoza, philosophe de l'amour*, Saint-Étienne: Publications de l'Université de Saint-Étienne.

Jaquet, C., P. Sévérac and A. Suhamy (eds) (2009), *La théorie spinoziste des rapports corps/esprit et ses usages actuels*, Paris: Hermann.

Laux, H. (1993), *Imagination et religion chez Spinoza*, Paris: Librairie philosophique J. Vrin.

Lazzeri, C. (ed.) (1999), *Puissance et impuissance de la raison*, Paris: Presses Universitaires de France.

Lécrivain, A. (1977–8), 'Spinoza et la physique cartésienne', *Cahiers Spinoza*. 1: pp. 235–65 and 2: pp. 93–206.

Macherey, P. (1978), *Hegel ou Spinoza*, Paris: Maspero.

Macherey, P. (1994–8), *Introduction à l'Éthique de Spinoza*, Paris: Presses Universitaires de France.

Matheron, A. (1969), *Individu et communauté chez Spinoza*, Paris: Éditions de Minuit.

Matheron, A. (1971), *Le Christ et le salut des ignorants chez Spinoza*, Paris: Aubier.

Matheron, A. (1986), *Anthropologie et politique au XVIIe siècle (Études sur Spinoza)*, Paris: Librairie philosophique J. Vrin.

Matheron, A. (1992), 'Passions et institutions chez Spinoza', in C. Lazzeri and D. Reynié (eds), *La Raison d'État: Politique et rationalité*, Paris: Presses Universitaires de France, pp. 141–70.

Matheron, A. (1994), 'L'indignation et le *conatus* de l'État spinoziste', in M. Revault d'Allonnes and H. Rizk (eds), *Puissance et ontologie*, Paris: Kimé, pp. 153–65.

Matheron, A. (1997), 'L'amour intellectuel de Dieu, partie éternelle de l'«amor erga Deum»', *Les Études philosophiques*, April–June 1997, pp. 231–48.

Méchoulan, H. (1990), *Amsterdam au temps de Spinoza*, Paris: Presses Universitaires de France.

Meinsma, O. (1983), *Spinoza et son cercle*, Paris: Librairie philosophique J. Vrin.

Mignini, F. (1983), *Introduzione a Spinoza*, Rome-Bari: Laterza.

Mignini, F. (1984–5), 'Sur la genèse du *Court Traité*: l'hypothèse d'une dictée originaire est-elle fondée ?', *Cahiers Spinoza*, 5, pp. 147–65.

Millet, L. (1970), *Pour connaître la pensée de Spinoza*, Paris-Montréal: Bordas.

Misrahi, R. (1972), *Le désir et la réflexion dans la philosophie de Spinoza*, Paris–London–New York: Gordon & Breach.

Misrahi, R. (1992a), *Le corps et l'esprit dans la philosophie de Spinoza*, Paris: Synthélabo.

Misrahi, R. (1992b), *Spinoza. Un itinéraire du bonheur par la joie*, Paris: Jacques Grancher.

Moreau, J. (1971), *Spinoza et le spinozisme*, Paris: Presses Universitaires de France.

Moreau, P.-F. (1975), *Spinoza*, Paris: Le Seuil.

Moreau, P.-F. (1994a), *L'expérience et l'éternité*, Paris: Presses Universitaires de France.

Moreau, P.-F. (1994b), 'Métaphysique de la gloire. Le scolie de la proposition 36 et le «tournant» du livre V', *Revue philosophique de la France et de l'étranger*, 184: 1, pp. 55–64.

Moreau, P.-F., C. Cohen-Boulakia and M. Delbraccio (eds) (2012), *Lectures contemporaines de Spinoza*, Paris: Presses de l'Université de Paris-Sorbonne.

Mugnier-Pollet, L. (1976), *La philosophie politique de Spinoza*, Paris: Librairie philosophique J. Vrin.

Ramond, C. (1995), *Qualité et quantité dans la philosophie de Spinoza*, Paris: Presses Universitaires de France.

Ramond, C. (1998), *Spinoza et la pensée moderne. Constitutions de l'objectivité*, Paris: L'Harmattan.

Rice, L. C. (1977), 'Emotion, Appetition and *Conatus* in Spinoza', *Revue internationale de philosophie*, 31: 119/120, pp.101–16.

Rousset, B. (1968), *La perspective finale de l'Éthique et le problème de la cohérence du spinozisme*, Paris: Librairie philosophique J. Vrin.

Saada, J. (1997), 'Le corps signe. Ordre des passions et ordre des signes: une économie du corps politique', in H. Giannini, P.-F. Moreau and P. Vermeren (eds), *Spinoza et la politique*, Paris: L'Harmattan, pp. 67–83.

Sévérac, P. (2005), *Le devenir actif chez Spinoza*, Paris: Honoré Champion.

Suhamy, A. (2010), *La communication du bien chez Spinoza*, Paris: Classiques Garnier.

Timmermans, B. (1994), 'Descartes et Spinoza: de l'admiration au désir', *Revue internationale de philosophie*, 48: 189(3), pp. 327–39.

Tosel, A. (1984), *Spinoza et le crépuscule de la servitude. Essai sur le Traité théologico-politique*, Paris: Aubier-Montaigne.

Totaro, G. (1994), '«Acquiescientia» dans la cinquième partie de l'*Éthique* de Spinoza', *Revue philosophique de la France et de l'étranger*, 184: 1, pp. 65–79.

Vandewalle, B., B. Busschaert and B. Meurin (2003), 'Des esprits animaux aux neurotransmetteurs, qui sait ce que peut le corps?', *XXXIIe Journées Annuelles de Thérapie Psychomotrice, Colloque Corps et culture*, Lille, 2 October 2003.

Vernière, P. (1954), *Spinoza et la pensée française avant la révolution*, Paris: Presses Universitaires de France.

Vinciguerra, L. (2005), *Spinoza et le signe, la genèse de l'imagination*, Paris: Librairie philosophique J. Vrin.

Voss, S. H. (1981), 'How Spinoza enumerated the affects', *Archiv für Geschichte der Philosophie*. 63: 2, pp. 167–79.

Wetlesen, J. (1979), *The Sage and the Way: Spinoza's Ethics of Freedom*, Assen: Van Gorcum.

Wolfson, A. H. (1934), *The Philosophy of Spinoza*, Cambridge, MA; London: Harvard University Press.

Wolfson, A. H. (1948), *Philo: Foundations of Religious Philosophy in Judaism, Christianity and Islam*, Cambridge, MA: Harvard University Press.

Yakira, E. (1989), *Contrainte, nécessité, choix. La métaphysique de la liberté chez Spinoza et Leibniz*, Zurich: Éditions du Grand Midi.

Yovel, Y. (1989), *Spinoza and Other Heretics*, Princeton: Princeton University Press.

Yovel, Y. (ed.) (1999), *Desire and Affect: Spinoza as a Psychologist*, New York: Little Room Press.

Zac, S. (1959), *La morale de Spinoza*, Paris: Presses Universitaires de France.

Zac, S. (1965), *Spinoza et l'interprétation de l'écriture*. Paris: Presses Universitaires de France.

Zac, S. (1979), *Philosophie, théolologie, politique dans l'œuvre de Spinoza*, Paris: Librairie philosophique J. Vrin.

Zourabichvili, F. (2002), *Spinoza, une physique de la pensée*, Paris: Presses Universitaires de France.

Zourabichvili, F. (2002), *Le conservatisme paradoxal de Spinoza*, Paris: Presses Universitaires de France.

Index

Alain (É. Chartier), 159
Alexander the Great, 51
Alquié, F., 79
Appuhn, C., 80, 81, 107, 139
Atlan, H., 2

Bacon, F., 153, 154
Beyssade, J.-M., 29n, 80n, 82n, 88,
    101, 102n, 127, 129n, 132,
    133
Bodin, J., 35
Busschaert, B., 3

Caillois, R., 79, 138
Changeux, J. P., 2, 7
Charron, P., 35
Cicero, M. T., 34, 76
Corneille, P., 80n
Cristofolini, P., 78n, 108
Curley, E. M., 78n, 81n, 107, 138

Damasio, A. R., 1, 4–7, 153, 154,
    155
Deleuze, G., 19
Descartes, R., 1, 4–6, 7, 11n, 27–46,
    47, 49, 51, 72, 73, 74, 75, 85,
    86, 91, 99, 125
Dominguez, A., 78n

Elisabeth of Bohemia, 5, 28
Elwes, R., 81n, 108

Giancotti, E., 78n, 87n, 108
Gueroult, M., 12

Hobbes, T., 57

Kant, I., 51

Leibniz, G. W., 12, 12n, 14, 19
Lordon, F., 3

Macherey, P., 39n, 80n, 108, 127n
Machiavelli, N., 32, 33, 46
Meurin, B., 3
Misrahi, R., 80n, 128, 129, 132
Montaigne, M., 35
Moreau, P.-F., 32n, 79

Ovid, 76n

Pappus, 38, 39
Parkinson, G. H. R., 78n, 108
Paul, 65, 66
Pautrat, B., 78n, 79n, 80n, 138
Peña Garcia, V., 78n

Quintus Curcius, Rufus, 58

Ricoeur, P., 2, 28
Rousset, B., 94

Schrijvers, M., 95n, 102, 110
Seneca, 34
Sévérac, P., 113n
Sévigné, Madame de, 81n
Shirley, S., 78n, 81n, 108, 138

Thomas Aquinas, 34, 35

Vandewalle, B., 3

Wetlesen, J., 110, 111n